'Tiger' Smith

of Warwickshire
and England

'Tiger' Smith

of Warwickshire
and England

The autobiography of E.J.Smith
as told to **Patrick Murphy**

READERS UNION
Group of Book Clubs
Newton Abbot 1981

This edition was published in 1981 by Readers Union by
arrangement with Lutterworth Press

Copyright © 1981 Patrick Murphy

Full particulars of RU are obtainable from
Readers Union Limited, P O Box 6, Newton Abbot,
Devon.

Printed in Great Britain
by Mackays of Chatham Ltd
for Readers Union

CONTENTS

Chapter   Page

1 Early days   1

2 Pre–1914 characters   11

3 1911–a memorable year   26

4 Australia   30

5 The Triangular Tournament   44

6 South Africa 1913/14   49

7 The post-war playing years   54

8 Tiger Smith—troublemaker?   69

9 Umpiring days   74

10 Coach for Warwickshire   89

11 World XI   96

12 Cricket today   106

13 Epilogue   115

Appendix. E. J. Smith's statistical record   117

Index   127

LIST OF PLATES
(between pages 88 and 89)

1 Three stalwarts of Warwickshire C.C.C.

2 E. J. Smith keeping wicket.

3 The Warwickshire team which won the County Cricket Championship in 1911.

4 Frank Foster.

5 The M.C.C. Touring Team to Australia for the 1911–12 Test series.

6 The menu card for the victory dinner, Sydney, 1912.

7 Percy Jeeves of Warwickshire and a cartoon of E. J. Smith.

8 Mr. & Mrs. J. H. Hearne and Mr. & Mrs. E. J. Smith. R. V. Ryder, Secretary of Warwickshire C.C.C.

9 1923 picture of the Warwickshire first team. Six famous names in Warwickshire cricket.

10 'Tiger' Smith in Barbados for the 1925–26 tour of West Indies.

11 Smith as umpire and as coach.

12 'Tiger' coaching in the Edgbaston Indoor Cricket School.

13 A 1956 picture of 'Tiger' in the changing rooms.

List of Plates

14 Alan Oakman, Jack Parsons and E. J. Smith.
   Three County champions: E. J. Smith, Dennis Amiss
   and Tom Pritchard.

15 'Tiger' talking cricket.

1
EARLY DAYS

I came into big-time cricket from the back streets of Birmingham. It'd be wrong to say I was brought up—dragged up would be a better description. I lost my parents at thirteen, leaving me to fend for myself. I was rough and ready then—I'm still rough and ready now—and in those days I really had to struggle.

Although I was 15 before I played my first serious cricket match, I'd been cricket mad since the day in 1896 when I watched Warwickshire play Kent at Edgbaston. No, I didn't pay at the gate, I watched the play from a tree outside the ground! I can still see J. R. Mason bowling to the Warwickshire skipper, H. W. Bainbridge while my brothers, mates and I clung for dear life to the tree branches.

I was hungry for cricket, but my school didn't play it so I was limited to scratch games in the park and playing in the street under the gas lamps. I was always the best bowler and the top batsman because I elected myself the skipper—oh, I was a fine player.

The turning point came when I left school and joined the Bournville Chocolate firm. Not that I thought so at the time—when I started at 13, I earned the princely sum of 5/10d for a 58-hour week. But at least I could play some sport. And one day, when I was 15, I played for the Bournville third team. It was the first day I kept wicket and I honestly found it easy. I'd gone along to watch my brother Harold play for the thirds when a message came through that the regular keeper was ill. I was roped in, given the pads and gloves and told to get on with it—and I had to look

1

lively when my brother hurled them down because he was
fast and could move the ball around. So I became a wicket-
keeper and loved it. I made the second team and wouldn't
play for the firsts. They were too flighty and full of airs and
anyway they were much older than I was. There was much
more fun in the second team, so there I stayed till I had a trial
with Worcestershire. I was recommended by the pro at
Bournville, Albert Bird, who played for the county. I was
17 and full of confidence because I found wicket-keeping a
most natural thing. Well, Worcestershire must have thought
so as well because they gave me a month's trial and asked
me to sign for them. But I'd been born in Warwickshire and
when they wrote to Edgbaston asking if I could go to New
Road, Warwickshire said 'no'. I didn't realize it at the time
but that letter changed my life because I was immediately
asked to have a trial for the county of my birth.

Presumably Warwickshire had heard about me on the
grapevine so in midsummer 1903 I turned up at Rugby to
play for the county Club and Ground. I'll never forget
seeing the wicket tended by a donkey pulling a roller between innings. Another thing that sticks in my memory—
the Warwickshire Secretary R. V. Ryder was in the Club
and Ground team. For the rest of our relationship over the
next quarter of a century, I suppose that was the only time
we ever had anything in common. . . .

I must have fared well because 'R.V.R.', as he was always
called, invited me to become a professional for Warwickshire. So an association that's lasted 75 years had begun and
although it's been a stormy relationship on occasions, I
wouldn't change anything if I had my time over again.

When I started at Edgbaston in the spring of 1904, I was
getting 25/– a week. Considering my last wage at Bournville
had been 16/– for a 60-hour week that started at 5.45 every
morning, I was happy. We were also paid every time we
played in the first team—£5 for a home game and £6 away
but then we had to find our own accommodation and pay
for that and our travelling expenses. So I was on my way. I

suppose even at 18 I must have been fairly cunning because I kept a secret from the committee at Edgbaston for years. I didn't want the committee to know I'd lost the top joints of the third and little fingers of my right hand and of the little finger of my left hand. I'd lost them in the Bournville factory when a machine chewed them off. I was 14 at the time and as it never affected my keeping for Bournville I didn't want the committee to have an excuse to get rid of me. So I kept mum and it wasn't until I got back from the 1911/12 Australia tour that anybody but my fellow-pros knew my secret. I was shaking hands with the county club's vice-chairman, Mr Howard Vaughton, when he noticed my fingers. 'Good God, Smith' he said in horror, 'where did you do that in Australia?' When I told him the truth, he said, 'if we'd known about that, we wouldn't have taken you on the staff.' So that was one time when it paid to keep my mouth shut. . . .

My first-class debut for Warwickshire was in that first season of 1904. It was against the touring South Africans and I can remember it as if it were yesterday. We lost by ten wickets against a team containing fine players like Sinclair, Kotze, Tancred and White. I batted number 11—the strongest in the side, holding all the others up—and I scored 0 not out and 8. I was annoyed when I was out in the second knock because I'd played quite well against the very fast bowler, Kotze. My skipper, J. F. Byrne, seemed set for a century and I held my end up for a time by playing Kotze off the front foot. The first time I went back—whoosh, I was beaten for speed and my castle was knocked over.

My first dropped catch was a costly one—it was off Sam Hargreave and the batsman, Louis Tancred, was 7 at the time. He went on to make 106. But dear old Sam shouted down the pitch, 'Never mind, young 'un, you'll miss a few more before you're finished'—and I did. . . .

I remember Billy Quaife bagging 'em in that match and a huge six from that great hitter, Jimmy Sinclair. He hit the ball out of the ground across the road and it landed in a tennis court, a carry of 150 yards. That's still the biggest hit I've seen.

I remember the reception I had from my skipper when we took the field. J. F. Byrne was waiting for me in the middle and instead of giving me some advice, he barked 'Get your flannels pressed, Smith. At least look like a cricketer even if you're not one yet.' Sam Hargreave put his arm round me and said 'Take no notice, young 'un, he'll come to you . . .' And he was right.

Dear old Sam was like a father to me in those early days. He took me under his wing and it was only when Sam had left the staff that I realized how much I owed him.

So I was reasonably happy with my first match and I played two more first-class games that season—against Cambridge University and Hampshire. The rest of the time I worked on the ground under Jack Bates. It was hard work—on match days we had to start work at 5 o'clock because all the grass cutting had to be done with horse-drawn machines and we had to fit the shoes on the horses. Then if there was no county game, we had to bowl at members in the nets till about 8 o'clock.

Yes, the young pro really knew his place in those days. I remember in my second season when I started work one day on the ground at five. I'd been slaving away for about four hours when 'R. V. R.' popped his head out of the window and said, 'You can give up now, Smith, you're playing today.' Someone dropped out through injury and I was on the field against Essex till 7 o'clock that night.

It was around this time that I picked up the nickname that's been with me ever since. And it all stemmed from that truculence and aggression I've always had. One day the youngsters were playing cards, waiting for the rain to stop. One picked on a small lad and accused him of cheating. A fight started, I laid out the big fellow and when he got up he didn't look so pretty. When the first team heard about it, Dick Lilley said 'We'll call him Tiger Smith'—a reference to a well-known boxer at that time. The name stuck and I suppose my gruff bark over the years has added to its meaning.

We pros kept our mouths shut even when we knew we were being treated badly. I remember at the end of my first season, I expected the £2 talent money every pro got for a first-team win. 'R.V.R.' wrote to tell me I was considered a junior still, so I would only get £1 bonus. But competition for a place on the staff was very strong, so you kept quiet. That's why our dressing-room was so bad—the committee knew we wouldn't complain. Normally about 7 or 8 pros would use the room which consisted of two washing basins, one toilet and no hot water. On cold days we'd all huddle round the little gas fire and if you wanted to dry your flannels out, you had to get there early. And when I left the staff in 1930, the conditions had hardly altered. . . .

When I first started at Edgbaston you had to take your own lunch. Otherwise, it'd cost 6d for a salad. At tea we'd get a mug each in our dressing-room. It used to cost about 6/6d for bed and breakfast, when you played away and that came out of your £6 match fee.

And all the while your place would be in jeopardy because of the amateurs. No matter how talented or promising the pro, if an amateur were available, he'd play instead. The game was still full of Sirs, Lords and a few Honourables and even though a lot of them weren't good enough, they still played whenever they wished.

This amateur dominance didn't really dawn on me until my second season. I only played six matches for the county in 1905 and just two in 1906. True, the great Dick Lilley was the established keeper but when he was away injured or on Test duty I was aware the amateurs were after my place. I got narky and told 'R.V.R.' what I thought. I didn't get any cash when playing for the Club and Ground and I'd heard another county wanted me.

So I told Sam Hargreave. Ryder wanted me to go to Lord's, I asked Sam's advice and he wrote to Lord's to see if I could join the M.C.C. staff. Within ten days I was playing for the M.C.C. and I remained on the Lord's staff until 1925. That's why I didn't play my first full season for Warwickshire till 1910. If my county wanted me to play for them they had to get permission from M.C.C. to release me. The competition at Lord's was really fierce—there were 55 pros who all played for their county, including Ewart Astill, Jack Newman, Alec Kennedy. It made me a better player because I saw all the Middlesex home matches and practised with players like J. T. Hearne, Frank Tarrant, Joe Hardstaff and Harry Butt. I kept my eyes open and couldn't help learning from men like Ranji, Reggie Spooner and C. B. Fry.

And the money was good, too. I was paid £4 a week, plus a match fee of £6 for a two-day match and £3 for one-day, and expenses. I used to bowl in the nets to the theatrical types like George Robey and Oscar Asche and they'd give me free passes for the theatre and healthy tips. Then after lunch I got more tips by bowling at the stockbrokers and the other toffs. I quickly learnt the ones with the cash and kept in with them.

In the winters I'd come back from London and try to find a job. But I was usually out of work and made sure my summer money lasted me. But I was happy and contented. I was learning the game and Warwickshire now knew they couldn't push me around.

Two things helped me break through at last for Warwickshire: the arrival of Frank Foster in 1908 and Dick Lilley's advancing years. Dick was a great keeper but by the time Foster started, his hands had taken a hammering. Foster with his speed off the wicket from a deceptively lazy run-up was a difficult man for Dick to face at his age, especially as there was a lot to take on the leg-side. Foster kept splitting the webbing of Dick's fingers and when it was clear that I could take Foster, Dick's days were numbered.

I kept in Foster's first match for the county, against Derbyshire. Within the first half-hour he clean bowled Cadman and L. G. Wright and he took six wickets in the match. In the next game at The Oval, I stumped Tom Hayward standing up on the leg-side to Foster. The Smith/Foster partnership had started . . .

Spare a thought for Dick Lilley, though he was as much a victim of poor equipment as advancing years. The gloves we had to wear in those days were very thin. They were made of felt, there was no padding, they were more like mittens so you had to take the ball correctly. And in those days keepers rarely stood back to a fast bowler—I stood up to Foster and Frank Field, Strudwick did to N. A. Knox at Surrey and Kent's Hubble and Huish did to Arthur Fielder. So the risk of finger injury was high, which meant you had to concentrate hard on 'giving' with the ball at the right time.

Cricket equipment was still fairly basic in the early part of the century. The wicket-keeper wore batsman's pads and there were hardly any 'boxes' until 1910. Before then the batsman stuffed towels inside the flannels if they expected to get hit in the groin but they were usually good enough to put bat to ball and not worry about getting hit. Well, the player that brought the abdominal protector into cricket was the great Johnny Tyldesley, who was hit in the groin while batting. Johnny was laid out and missed the next six weeks. When he came back he'd marketed the first authentic 'box'. So next time you cricketers slip one inside your flannels, spare a thought for poor Johnny Tyldesley that day. . . .

Yes, we keepers had to be tough in those days. I think I was the first to tape some of my fingers together so that they wouldn't break. And only once in my career did I get a finger injury—when I broke the second finger of my left hand trying to catch Gilbert Jessop down the leg side off Frank Foster. That happened on the Friday but I still kept against Worcester on the Monday with a little pad stuck between the first and second finger.

I'm often asked about the differences between today's cricket and the time when I started. Well there are many, some of them for the good but others for the worse. Take the bowler's run-ups, for example. I can't believe my eyes today when I see bowlers running forty yards and delivering the ball at medium pace. When I first kept for Warwickshire I never saw anybody with a longer run than fifteen yards. None of the fast men—Walter Brearley, N. A. Knox, Dick Burrows, Arthur Fielder among them—took a long run, they all had good actions and straight run-ups, none of this curving nonsense. There wasn't any swearing on the field, either. The pros were too frightened of the amateurs to step out of line. It was, 'yes sir' and 'no, sir' and 'good morning, sir'. I always tried to keep out of the way of the amateurs because they weren't bothered about me, and although I respected the cricket abilities of some of them, I never wanted to get close to them.

Many modern players think the old 'uns were proper boozers. That's not true, although I remember one match against Leicestershire in 1905 when drink played a decisive role. We needed about 30 to win at one stage with five wickets in hand when the Leicestershire fast bowler, George Gill, went off the field. A few minutes later, he was back, bowling like a demon; he finished with four wickets and we lost by 9 runs! We later found out that George had himself a quick wash-down, swigged three brandies and felt much better for it. The big-wigs at Lord's got to hear about it, *Wisden* made a stiff comment about George going off for 'a rest', and an edict was passed that no player could go off for 'a massage' during play.

All the fast bowlers loved a drink—Arnold Warren, Alex Skelding, Billy Bestwick and dozens more would have a couple of pints before play so they could sweat freely. That way they didn't sap any energy. But they certainly weren't boozers—they were hard, fit men doing a strong man's job.

And it'll probably come as a surprise to those who know my fondness for a drink that I was a teetotaller till I was twenty five, and I only came to drink because I was ill one day while playing. I felt a bit dicky, a doctor was summoned

8

and he told me to have some Guinness and a few boiled eggs. I felt much better afterwards and since then I've enjoyed many a pint—purely for medicinal purposes, you understand. But one thing I swear—Tiger Smith was never unfit for play. Towards the end of my career I'd have a glass of beer before the start of play but I was always fit for cricket.

What were the other major differences between then and now? Well we used to start matches on Monday and Thursday. Seems daft now, I agree, but county treasurers only woke up to the fact that they were missing gate money when the 1909 Test at Edgbaston finished on the Saturday morning, the last day. Warwickshire were the first to start on Saturdays so that even if play was held up, the club could still make money through the turnstiles. It seems unbelievable now but it wasn't till 1920 that Saturday starts applied to all first class games over the weekend.

We didn't play all the counties in the Championship, either, in many cases because of feuds dating back years. We didn't play Kent between 1899 and 1913, Sussex wouldn't play us for a long time because they thought we'd poached Billy Quaife from them, but the most hilarious feud involved Essex. They weren't pleased because Teddy Diver chose to make a gesture when he skippered Warwickshire at Leyton one year. You see, Teddy was a pro at the time and to his and his colleagues' delight no amateur was available for us that match. So Teddy decided to have some fun at the expense of all the fuddy-duddies who saw to it that the amateurs ruled the roost. He marched his team in single file out of the pros gate and strode in step to the amateurs gate. Once they got there they marched on the spot, then turned at right angles and the team strode out to the wicket, still in single file with great grins on their faces. The pros had made the point that for once they were in charge and Essex took a dim view of the demonstration. So did Warwickshire—and although Teddy was a fine batsman the club waited for an excuse to get rid of him and when he obliged by being cited in a divorce case shortly afterwards, he was out.

In those days the Edgbaston ground was much smaller than the impressive match stadium you see today. It could only hold about 5,000 at the turn of the century. An average game would attract about 2,000 but there were often crowds of about 10,000 to the larger grounds like Hove, Trent Bridge and Manchester—and this just for county matches.

Another thing that was rare—a county coach. At Edgbaston we had the legendary Alfred Shaw with us for three weeks at the start of the season, then he went on to Worcester. The rest of the time we young players had to develop by watching and listening. You had to work things out for yourself; there was no one around to hold your hand and overwhelm you with theories. It was a hard school—but a happy one.

2
PRE-1914 CHARACTERS

The period before the Great War was dominated by the amateurs. Of course there were some great professional players but it wasn't unusual for sides to have seven amateurs, particularly the metropolitan ones like Middlesex who could claim those who combined playing with business in the City. Overall I'd say the amateur's influence on the game was a good one. They didn't have to worry about keeping their places so they could play their shots and please the crowd. And because of their public school background they could instil discipline into the pros.

But the amateur dominance led to some strange goings-on. There was the time in 1909 when a brewer called Russell Everitt played his first game for us at The Oval. He captained the side because apart from the young Frank Foster there was no other amateur in the team—even though he didn't know much about us and there were far more knowledgeable cricketers in the pros' dressing-room.

Many of the amateurs got away with cheating because some umpires were frightened of being thrown off the list. It was interesting to see how many amateurs got the benefit of the doubt with catches behind the wicket or lbw appeals, especially the captains, because they were the ones with the power over umpires due to the reports they'd file to Lord's. I well remember Lord Hawke batting against us for Yorkshire. I caught him and the straightforward appeal was upheld by the umpire. The conversation then went like this:

> Lord Hawke: 'What did you say?'
> Umpire: 'Not out, sir'

And my skipper, J. F. Byrne, told me off for complaining!

The amateur's status was once unwittingly summed up for me by Lord Dalmeny, who was then the captain of Surrey. 'Good morning, Tiger' he said as we met in the middle. 'Good morning, my Lord' said I, and then encouraged by his mood, I said, 'Just right for cricket,' only to be stopped short by the words: 'Twice a day, good morning and good night—that's enough for me!'

W. G. Grace was the most famous player of that age and deservedly so, considering what he did for the game in the eyes of the public and the bad wickets he had to bat on. He skippered me several times for the M.C.C. and I always tried to keep out of his way. Once when our side was doing badly he was having a gin with Len Braund at the bar and Len pointed out that I batted higher up for my county. 'Why didn't you tell me?' he demanded in that curious, high-pitched voice. 'Because you're the captain, not me' said I—as if he would have taken any notice of advice from someone like me. 'Put your pads on, you're in next,' came the demand. I batted well and W.G. said 'Next time you play for me, tell me where you want to bat.' If I hadn't stood up to him he'd have dominated me: I'd seen him do that to many a young player. The umpires were afraid of him—if he came back today he'd spend a lot less time at the crease.

Then there was that other martinet, C. B. Fry. In fact I found him a proper autocrat. A marvellous batsman with great front-foot power, he was a fine scholar who didn't suffer fools easily. He wasn't a good captain—he didn't understand our feelings for a start and there were times on the field when he seemed in a world of his own. Once in the Lord's Test against South Africa in 1912 he behaved remarkably. Charlie Llewellyn had a swipe against Syd Barnes and it went miles up in the air. Fry was at short leg and it was a dolly catch for him, but he went round in a circle

12

waiting for the ball and when it came down Fry was yards away, having run himself dizzy. He was so embarrassed he pulled the peak of his cap round to the back of his neck and disappeared into the long field, a strange place for the captain to go. As luck would have it, a ball was skied out to him soon afterwards and he ran the other way and a simple catch went begging. I don't know what he was up to but I've never seen such behaviour from a skipper before—and this in a Test Match. But Fry was quick-witted. He knew how to put someone down and once he put Walter Brearley in his place. It was a Test Trial, the first of the season with another to come at Lord's before we took on the Australians and the South Africans that summer. Bert Relf was batting and I was standing up to Walter, who was bowling fast. Walter, great-hearted trier that he was, felt offended I was behind the stumps and called out, 'You won't stand up to me at Lord's, Tiger.' Came Fry's reply from mid-on: 'Have you chosen yourself then, Walter?' Walter didn't say much after that. . . .

If Fry and W.G. were autocrats, another great amateur, Gilbert Jessop, was a real gentleman. He was straight as a die, honest and thoughtful to the pros. And what a cricketer! His natural ability was great—he could bowl really fast, his batting was marvellously entertaining and his fielding spectacular. The hardest return I've had to field behind the stumps was from Gilbert, and it came in from 100 yards! It was at Leeds in 1912 against the South Africans. He threw in from the very long boundary at the pavilion end and the ball nearly knocked me off my feet. It came in as hard as if Jack Hobbs had thrown in from cover point and the only similar speed I've experienced was when I first kept to Harold Larwood.

His batting was unique: his eye and reflexes amazing, he simply played the ball to its length. He could cut, late cut, work you round to fine leg, and with a cross bat drive you straight. His stance was amazing: he wouldn't bother with a guard, he'd put his bat in line with the middle and off stumps and then crouch down so low that the bowler couldn't see the wicket. If he came back today many would say he was no use because of his crouching stance yet how well I remember a century he got against us at Edgbaston. In his innings I never took a ball, he simply didn't let one past his bat. The crowds loved him. In Birmingham the newspaper placards would say 'Jessop not out at lunchtime' and there'd be an extra 2,000 in the ground in the afternoon. When he came in to bat, we never had specific plans to get him out. We'd keep the normal field with the fielders positioned slightly deeper and try to get him to play wide and stretch. Nobody bowled his guts out at Jessop, there was just no point. If he was in the mood, you'd had it, so we'd enjoy his innings almost as much as the crowd. And if anyone did bounce a few at him, they knew about it when Jessop was bowling because he could look after himself and bowl very fast bouncers.

About 5ft. 7in. tall with strong, square shoulders, Gilbert Jessop was one of the all-time greats and he'd flourish in any era of cricket.

Another great gentleman was Victor Trumper. I got to know him well on the 1911–12 tour of Australia and I don't think a kinder man ever lived. He wouldn't see anyone starve and was so generous to kids who came into his sports shop with hard luck stories. When I kept to him in Australia he only had three years to live; he was tubercular then and coughing a little when he batted, but he never complained. The off-field incidents in the Australians dressing-room saddened Victor. Stronger men like Warwick Armstrong pressurised him into supporting the players' demands to have Frank Laver as their manager on the forthcoming tour of England. So Victor didn't come to England in 1912 and I think he was bewildered by it all. He'd also heard that some of the Test selectors didn't rate him all that highly, yet he got a beautiful hundred against us in the first Test and fifty in the last. In that last Test, Victor turned to me at one stage and said, 'Tiger, they think I'm finished.' All I could think was, 'I wish I could play like you, Victor.'

One example of his sportsmanship on that tour. He was

captaining an Australian XI against us and Jack Hearne skied a ball to J. N. Crawford off Roy Minnett. Jack was walking to the pavilion when Victor called him back because someone in the crowd had shouted 'no ball' when Jack was about to play his shot. Can you see a skipper doing something like that today?

A very superstitious man, Victor. If he got runs wearing a particular pair of trousers or using a special bat, nothing would persuade him to change either. As a result Victor's bat was normally black with age.

Like Jack Hobbs, I don't think he had a weakness in his batting, apart from his ill-health. A most un-Australian person, to me he was a champion and one of the most endearing men I've ever met.

'Endearing' is never the adjective used to describe the great Sydney Barnes. He was a rough diamond who spoke his mind and as a result put many peoples' backs up. Not surprisingly, because I was of similar temperament, Barney and I always got on very well. On the first day of that famous Melbourne Test in 1911–12, Barney had a brush with the manager, Major Pawley. Barney had just come off the field at lunch after turning in one of the great Test bowling performances of all time and he fancied a drink. 'I'll have a bottle of wine,' he said to the pavilion attendant and I sat down with him. Pawley overheard, popped his head round the door and said, 'We haven't catered for wine, you know, Syd,' to which Barney replied: 'I didn't ask you. I want wine and I'll pay for it'—and in those days a professional didn't speak like that to the manager. But Barney got away with it and the two of us polished off the bottle before going out on to the field.

And Barney was at it again in the afternoon session. He was so incensed by some terrible umpiring that he put his foot on the ball and refused to bowl again until the boos and the catcalls from the crowd stopped. He did bowl again, but he'd made his point.

Then on the 1913–14 tour to South Africa, he got away

with something that most pros wouldn't think of trying. His wife and son had come out with him at his expense (none of the amateurs followed suit) and he asked to go home early, which meant missing the last Test. Now Barney had been the main reason why we'd won the rubber so easily—he'd taken 49 wickets in the first four Tests—and presumably this was why he got his own way. So while the cricket world thought he was nursing an injured knee, Barney was steaming happily home with his family!

Barney's confidence was always high. Asked once why he didn't bowl the googly on that all-conquering South African tour, he replied disdainfully: 'I didn't find it necessary.' He could bowl everything—he weighed the batsman up as he came in and tried to get him out right at the start. If he survived Barney would start analysing him, he'd look at the position of the batsman's hands on the handle to see if he was an on- or an off-side player and then he'd play on any weakness he'd spotted. He had long fingers and he could really spin the ball if necessary—at medium pace. His action was superb—he used to carry the ball in the left hand so the batsman didn't know what he was bowling and then at the start of the final leap he'd transfer the ball to the right hand. He bowled immaculately to his field; when he bowled leg-breaks he'd station a point because he thought that if the batsman had a swing and miscued, it would go to point rather than on the leg side. And he was often right.

He wanted his own way, it's true. If the skipper wouldn't let him have his own field, he'd refuse to bowl. But I never found him any trouble—he was no more awkward than I was or a few others I could mention.

George Gunn was another of the great characters in the professional ranks at that time. George liked nothing better than getting under the crowd's skin. Once in Australia, he continued batting after breaking a bone in his hand. The crowd jeered him for slow scoring, but George loved it. I honestly think George could do anything he wanted on the cricket field once he put his mind to it. I remember once at

Trent Bridge, he told us the committee weren't happy with his run of low scores so he was going to get a century that day. He did. It took him a long time and contained 77 singles. In the second innings he told us at the start that he'd been criticized for his slow scoring, so he'd get a fast hundred that day. He did—it took him just over two hours.

George was so casual—he'd walk around as if next week would do. He was the best player of fast bowling I've ever seen. I've seen him walk down the wicket to really fast bowlers like Ted McDonald and drive them back over their heads. I've never watched anyone with more time to play the ball and as a slip fielder, he was brilliant. He'd catch screamers with either hand, chuckle and throw the ball back as if it was the easiest thing in the world. He was so confident; after the googly bowler H. V. Hordern bowled us to defeat in the Sydney Test in 1911 George calmly announced that in the next Test he would put a halt to such tactics. He was right. He kept walking down the pitch to Hordern and playing him away, until the exasperated bowler said to him, 'Why don't you come and take the ball out of my hand?'

He always had a smile on his face, was always relaxed and never forced his company on anyone. He was immaculate in everything he did, his clothes and cricket gear were always spotless. And if you gave George a piano he'd keep you up all night, with beautiful renditions of arias and other classical works.

Not many people know it but George prevented a tragedy in 1907 when the England team were sailing to Australia. George hadn't been selected and was going to Australia for his health (although he subsequently *did* play). Anyway, one Saturday night on board ship, George sauntered up on deck and there was the England captain, A. O. Jones in a trance trying to climb over the rail. George said to his county captain, 'What are you doing?' and Jones replied, 'Oh, just going for a walk.' For years afterwards, George couldn't explain what got into Jones. He wasn't drunk and he was a very stable man. It was simply a mental blackout but imagine the explanations that would have been demanded by Lord's if George hadn't decided on a breath of fresh air that night. . . .

One of the great drinking men of that period was that fine all-rounder Len Braund. He could really hold his drink but if you ended up with Len you'd be out all night and few of us could stand the strain.

I remember once I went on an M.C.C. tour of Norfolk with Len and we had a great time; or rather Len had a great time because he wasn't sober all that often during it. We were due to play at Yarmouth on the Monday, so Harry Storer, Billy Coleman and myself waited for hours at Liverpool Station for Len on the Sunday. When play started the next day, there was no Len. I of all people had to bowl from the start till lunchtime and then just before lunch Len turned up in a cab with a porter carrying his bag. And he was well oiled. The skipper said to him, 'I suppose we'd better get someone out, Braund' and tossed him the ball; Len let it drop to the ground and caught it with his feet shaped like a 'V', all the while grinning from ear to ear. In three overs he bowled out five men with some really fast bowling and then he made 160 superb runs before the close of play. He was sweating like a bull but he really sobered up quickly.

On the same tour he met up with Tommy Fishwick, the old Warwickshire player, when we played at Hunstanton. Tommy was secretary then of the local golf club and so Len could have a few drinks with his old pal. He fooled the rival skipper into thinking it was far too windy to play before lunch!

Another of the piano-playing brigade, Len would bash away at it all night.

There were many characters at Edgbaston before the Great War but the influence of two men—Dick Lilley and Frank Foster—was very strong.

Dick Lilley was one of the most knowledgeable cricketers I've known. He'd learned a lot from Archie MacLaren with the England team and I picked up many tips just watching him in my early days. He was so unfussy and solid and in all the time I watched him, I never saw him on his backside; he knew just how far he could reach behind the stumps.

He was a serious man who kept himself very much to himself. A fine rifle shot, he won the gold stick at Monte Carlo while still playing. He won a lot of money there but he then blew it on the gambling tables. A very abstemious man, he kept a pub while still a player.

Dick only ever gave me two pieces of advice—to forget about dropped catches and to save overthrows by getting to the returns from the field. I thought he could have offered me more tips but I was in a very delicate situation and I thought he resented competition from the young keeper.

The trouble really blew up in the 1911 season when we won the Championship. By then I was keeping regularly and Dick was playing as batsman. We were at Harrogate against Yorkshire and David Denton came in to bat. Without consulting Frank Foster, his skipper, Dick started waving several fielders into deeper positions. Dick knew that David could play the lofted cover-drive but Foster was furious because the spectators could hear Dick ordering the fielders around. Foster said to Dick: 'I'll take your advice if you come to me, but don't make me look a fool.'

In that same match, I had another shock. Foster said to me: 'You're keeping wicket well, considering you were out till three in the morning.' Astonished, I said, 'Who told you that?' Foster said 'Dick Lilley.' The truth was that I'd been up at three taking off Dick's leg bandages that he needed for his varicose veins—and I'd hardly had a drink!

Dick's differences of opinion with his team-mates and the captain marked a sad end to a great career and I thought Warwickshire were unfair to him when they left him off the team picture when we won the title that year. He'd done so much for the county that at least he deserved to be acknowledged.

Frank Foster was, above all, the cricketer who made me. I

was the only one that could take him easily, even though many others were tried out in the Test trials. He had this lovely easy action off a six-yard, loping run and he was really quick off the pitch. He was tall—nearly six foot—and he let the ball go from high up. He had a very loose bowling arm and when he brought that arm over, he really whacked it down and the batsmen were constantly surprised by his speed off the pitch.

He was a natural, uncomplicated cricketer. I never saw him in the nets at Edgbaston. He'd just stroll on to the pitch and look a fine all-rounder and a good slip. His confidence was amazing—he'd take on a bet at any time about his next innings or his next piece of bowling. Once at Edgbaston he clean bowled that fine Worcestershire batsman, H. K. Foster. He said he wasn't ready so Frank shrugged his shoulders—and clean bowled him again two balls later.

I remember a match against Yorkshire in 1911. George Hirst and Alonzo Drake were both in the eighties and George turned to me and said, 'You know Tiger, I can't understand how this Foster gets so many lbws.' Frank was beside me at slip, I told him this and he said, 'I'll show him.' The next over he came on, and the first ball came back and hit George on the backside. The next ball straightened—it pitched on middle and leg and knocked his off peg over. 'Did that straighten, George?' I grinned. 'Ay, lad, it did,' he said. And in the second innings Foster got George lbw!

If you played back to Foster you really had to look sharp. He left C. B. Fry's left thigh looking like a piece of liver after one Test trial. He laid out Fanny Walden once. They had to put ice packs round him—all this off a six-yard ambling run.

I'm often asked Foster's real speed. Well, he was quicker than either Gary Sobers or Alan Davidson because his run-up was so deceptive.

I honestly never found Foster difficult to keep to. For one so young, his accuracy was impressive. After sighting him for the first couple of overs I always stood up to him—and this made my name. Before the third Test at Adelaide in 1912 Plum Warner said to me, 'How are we going to get Clem Hill out?' I said, 'Stumped Smith, bowled Foster.' And he was—for a duck. We'd got a plan and we played to it. Then in 1912 in a Test trial, Warner asked how we'd get Phil Mead out. My answer was the same: 'Stumped Smith bowled Foster.' And he was—three times out of four innings in the trials, Mead was out to the Foster/Smith combination. No wonder Frank got me in the Test side.

We never had a pre-arranged signal for a stumping. His normal line was middle and leg and I'd stand there. I'd say something like 'Down the leg side whenever you're ready' between overs and I was there for it when it came.

As a captain it was a pleasure to play for him. He was only twenty-two when he became skipper and he had a lot of trouble with Dick Lilley, but he stood up to him manfully. He was a fanatic for brighter cricket and he'd always accept a challenge.

As a batsman he was very entertaining. He loved to hit the ball and I well remember an enjoyable partnership with him at Dudley in 1914 when he hit 305 against Worcestershire. We added 166 in 70 minutes and I was caught and bowled by an amateur called A. T. Cliff—I hit that one so hard that if he hadn't caught it, I'd have been had up for manslaughter!

He was handsome, dashing, a real ladies' man. He was nearly lost to cricket as early as 1910 because he was going to marry a girl but she jilted him, so his loss was Warwickshire's gain. A brilliant billiards player, he over-reached himself and lost a lot of money to the professional players. He never did very well on the horses, either.

His life was one of anti-climax after his success in Australia. He had a motor bike accident in 1914 and the foot injury he suffered prevented him playing again. In the end he fell on hard times but I shall always remember with fondness the cheerful, confident young all-rounder who helped me play for England.

Billy Quaife was another character at Edgbaston. A small, spare man, he was remarkably fit. He was still playing for the county at 55 (he scored a century on his last appearance) and he played hockey for the county till he was 53. After playing cricket all day he'd go home and play a couple of sets of tennis. He was an example to us all and I don't think the committee really appreciated him until he'd left.

Billy was at his best when the score was 13 for 2 and he had to pull the side round. He was the best defensive player I've seen and I used to love batting with him to watch his footwork. He was a placer and a glider with a great late-cut. He played forward mostly and despite being just 5ft. 6in. he played the fast men really well. He didn't bother about getting behind the line, he played them on a parallel line so that he could choose which angle to play the ball.

He was only hit once by a fast bowler—by Yorkshire's Abe Waddington in the ribs—so his technique must've been sound. Many critics said he was too slow yet if he was playing today I guarantee you that because of his sure selection of strokes and footwork he'd be one of England's fastest scorers.

At 55 he was still a fine cover point—a point that wasn't lost on two of his team-mates from earlier years. Both Sid Santall and Charlie Baker valued their hands for their jobs—Charlie was a cartoonist and Sid a clerk in the winter—and whenever the ball came near either of them in the air they'd shout 'Yours Billy'. And the faithful Billy would cover yards to do their job for them.

A strict teetotaller was Billy, but he'd always be happy with a cup of tea and a natter about the game. Only once did he ever take alcohol. He was batting and asked me to get him a drink because he wasn't feeling well. I got him a drop of brandy, he took one nip—and then went on to a double-century.

I respected Billy's principles about drink so much that I once got in a row with someone on a train. I was going to London for a Test Trial and I overheard a man say that the reasons for Billy Quaife's recent poor form were 'the usual ones—women and wine'. I told him who I was and that he was talking rubbish and he closed up like a tinpot. Afterwards he bought me a gin and tonic as an apology. . . .

Billy was an interesting off-break bowler with a suspicious kink in his elbow at times. So the famous Australian umpire, Jim Phillips, was sent to no-ball him. But Billy realized what he was up to, stuck to leg-breaks instead. Jim growled 'You little devil, you've done me', and we all had a good laugh about it.

One of the shrewdest professionals, Billy was never short of money. He was in partnership with Dick Lilley in a sports business and at one stage they went to court in a dispute. The judge told them they were better cricketers than businessmen and eventually Billy bought out Dick.

A man of high principle, Billy was a great servant to Warwickshire. And how many current batsmen do you know averaging 66 for a whole season yet unable to get into the England side?

The two pros I was closest to at Edgbaston were Crowther Charlesworth, a fine batsman, and Sam Hargreave, the slow bowler. They were older than me and took me under their wing at the start, probably because they realized I was like them—a rough diamond. Charlesworth was a real character. He loved wild animals, flowers and the smell of the country. He'd go out into the country if he wasn't playing cricket, sit on a gate all day, say 'How do' to everyone and be as happy as a sandboy.

After a couple of pints he'd be a real handful and his poor wife never knew when to expect him home—if at all. Because he could never be sure when he'd get home Charlesworth would bring food to the pros' dressing-room and cook it there. Trouble was, he'd often forget about it. One day early in the season there was a strange smell. Charlesworth said 'Oh, that'll be my grub'—he opened the locker and there was this mildewed packet of Shredded Wheat and a haddock that was going back to sea, left over from last season.

He was a rough diamond with a big heart, and after coaching at Dartmouth Naval College he died in a Salvation Army hostel in Yorkshire. He was larger than life and a man I'll never forget.

Sam Hargreave was another who loved a laugh. Once Dick Lilley bagged 'em at Bristol and Sam put a couple of rabbits in his bag. Dick wasn't pleased! Then there was the time J. F. Byrne, the skipper, put that natural number eleven Frank Field in at number 10 and Sam was last man. Sam responded by locking Frank in the toilet and going out at number 10. . . .

A naturally kind man, Sam would often put his arm round me, call me 'young 'un' and sympathize. He taught me a lot of things that I used when I became a coach. He became a bookie and died of cancer when he was just 53. I missed him badly and my only consolation was that he died proud of me.

Jack Parsons was a Warwickshire player with a varied life; he started as a pro, won the MC in the Great War, became a captain in the Indian Army and then was ordained to the ministry after looking after his mother on her death bed. When he first started at Edgbaston he'd cycle from Coventry to the ground and back for practices—a round trip of forty miles.

Standing over six feet, he was a fearsome straight-driver. He couldn't cut a loaf of bread so you'd try to get him on the back foot, but if you dropped it slightly short he'd drive it back straight. I remember two incidents concerning Jack's driving. He was in his early seventies when he came with me to Lilleshall to talk about coaching. Walter Robins was there, and Gubby Allen and Harry Altham, all of them supervising, and they demonstrated a method of improving straight-driving. They'd drop the ball off a chair and ask the batsman to drive it. Old Jack did it beautifully and they were all flabbergasted at his upright stance and clean hitting.

Then at 75 he came to the nets at Edgbaston. I was in charge of the indoor school and he asked if the kids could bowl at him. They thought he was easy meat but within a couple of minutes they were ducking and weaving out of the way. It was wonderful to roll back the years and see that superb straight driving again.

Jack could look after himself too. Once when Yorkshire were playing us, George Macaulay was cutting up rough, pretending to throw the ball at the batsman's stumps as he followed through. Jack shouted at him, 'If you throw it, I'll be coming up to see you' and George took the hint.

Then there was Sep Kinneir, the left-hand bat. Sep was a lovely lad but although sturdy he was anaemic and he missed almost a complete season because of it. He was always smoking his pipe and that can't have been good for him. Sep was a staunch Socialist and he was always arguing with Sid Santall, who was a strong Tory. In those days pros weren't expected to talk about politics, least of all own up to being a Socialist.

Sep was the first man to bring a motorbike on to the ground—which prompted a member of the committee to say that the professionals were being paid too much, a remark that tells you a lot about the committee, I hope. Ironically he died on his motor bike—of a heart attack while on the way back from a game of golf. He was only 57.

Frank Field was our great-hearted fast bowler in my early days. He loved a joke, never had a serious thought in his head, but was a captain's dream. He suffered badly from strains. Every morning he'd get down to the ground early, sip a tot of whisky and massage his elbow. In those days there was no such thing as a physiotherapist; you had to do the massaging yourself. Frank would bowl even if half-fit and I don't think I've known a greater trier.

Great names, great times. It was a golden era and I'm proud to have been a part of it. There were hardships, of course, and we professionals didn't get the respect I think we deserved but in the long run we were all getting paid for what we loved best—playing cricket.

3
1911—A MEMORABLE YEAR

The year 1911 stands out in my life as the most memorable
one. I started that season as a 25-year old wicketkeeper for
an average county. I ended it as England's keeper against
Australia with a County Championship medal and my first
hundred under my belt.

And yet when that season started I'd no ambitions other
than to play for my county. I'd never thought of playing for
England; there was no lack of competition from men like
Herbert Strudwick, Ernie Bale and Joe Murrell, and
anyway I was playing for an unfashionable county which
was never watched by the selectors. I reckoned without the
success of Frank Foster that season. At 22 he skippered us to
our first title, did the double and bowled devastatingly in
the Test trials. And it soon became clear that no other
keeper could take him as well as I could—they just
couldn't pick up his leg-and-middle line. So looking back I
suppose it was inevitable that if Foster played for England
so would Smith— although that never occurred to me at
the time.

There were several reasons for our title success, apart
from Foster's dynamic captaincy. It was a hot, dry summer
which suited our fast bowling attack of Field, Foster and
Santall. If it'd been a wet summer we would have struggled
because we had no class spinner. We scored runs quickly,
thanks to Foster, Jack Parsons and Crowther Charlesworth,
and in Kinneir, Foster and Parsons we had a very fine trio of
slips. And we were lucky—we pipped Kent by 0·16 of a
point and we played six fewer games than Kent that season

and didn't even play them. But we were well led and always went for a win.

It wasn't the happiest side I'd played in, despite our success. There were too many jealousies. The Dick Lilley incidents left a sour taste in the mouths of many of us and Kinneir and Santall often argued too much about politics. But there's no doubt we played attractive cricket and pleased the crowds. And the talent money came in handy—we pros shared £300 between us.

The team was delighted to prove one person wrong in 1911. After our first match at The Oval, when we were thrashed by Surrey, the newspaper critic, E. H. D. Sewell, a former Essex player, wrote that we weren't even a good second eleven.

Sewell had neglected to mention we were without Frank Foster in that match and that we were caught on a devil of a wet wicket, but it stung us and we set out to prove him wrong.

I've always thought the turning point came at Old Trafford when we won by 137 runs. For almost the only time in my career the sun shone at Old Trafford for three days and we played well with the sun on our backs. Then, after a few midsummer setbacks, we ended up with nine wins and three draws, giving us 54 points out of a possible sixty. And that's Championship form.

I've got so many vivid memories of that long, hot season. There was the match at Harrogate where Frank Foster refused to play unless another wicket was cut. He said the wicket had been watered deliberately at one end to suit Wilfred Rhodes and he was so annoyed that he bowled like a demon and Yorkshire were all out for 58. The wicket was, to say the least, sporting, and I well recall David Denton saying to the next man, 'Get thi' pads on quick, I've got a wife and three kids at home.' And their skipper, Sir Archibald White, was caught off his elbow—he didn't wait to see if the appeal was upheld, he was off like a shot!

Then there was the game against Surrey that gave me my

first hundred. I went in as nightwatchman and typical of me, I hit a six before close of play. I got the runs very quickly the next day and I can still see the ball that helped me reach three figures. It was from 'Razor' Smith, it was on the leg side, I went to pull it and it went down to fine leg for a boundary. Tom Hayward complained: 'Why bowl him one on the leg side when he's 99?', but I was walking on air, it was a thrilling feeling.

After that innings, I moved up to number 8 and I continued trying to hit the cover off the ball. Luckily my skipper encouraged me to do just that.

I was then selected for the Players v the Gentlemen at Lords and must've fared well because a few days later I was sent a telegram asking if I was available for the tour of Australia.

We were at Chichester playing Sussex and I was astonished and proud, especially as many other fine keepers were passed over. Herbert Strudwick was to be the other keeper and I had no doubts that he was to be number one on the tour. I was also pleased to learn that my two county colleagues, Sep Kinneir and Frank Foster, had also been selected so I wouldn't lack company.

But there was still the Championship to be won before I could dream of Australia. We achieved this by beating Northamptonshire in the final game. We had to win this one to take the title, and apart from anxious moments when it rained there was never any doubt. They were all out for 73 in their first knock and it took just 35 minutes to polish them off on the final morning. So it was champagne all the way back to Birmingham and then a reception in the Grand Hotel.

But we soon came down to earth when, as Champion County, we played The Rest at The Oval. We were hammered. With players like Spooner, Hobbs, Mead, Warner, Fry, Rhodes and Woolley in their side, they made 631 for five. I was pleased with myself, though, I let only five byes through in that innings. And it was during that innings that I had an interesting insight into the mind of Pelham Warner. With his score on 180 he turned to me and said, 'You know, I've never made a double-hundred before.' Shortly afterwards I missed stumping him off W. C. Hands. I didn't realize he was out of his ground and I just collected the ball and threw it back to the bowler. But I certainly didn't let Warner off the hook, even though he was like a small boy with excitement at the prospect of getting a double-hundred. I've often wondered since whether Warner thought well of me after that incident. Especially when I found out that he'd made two previous double centuries! Afterwards, Frank Foster told me that Warner had asked several people what they thought of me as a person before selecting me for the tour. I'd hate to think Plum thought I was one of his pets now that I'd missed stumping him.

But I wasn't concerned what the amateurs thought of me. I just kept out of their way as much as possible and concentrated on preparing for the trip of a lifetime.

4
AUSTRALIA

I've got so many memories of that famous tour, most of them happy ones. There was the bowling of Barnes and Foster, the masterly batting of Jack Hobbs, the pleasure of playing against Victor Trumper, the good-natured barracking from the large crowds and the thrill of hammering Australia 4–1. I'll never forget the terrible umpiring on that tour or the numerous rows between the Australian players and their selectors. But my abiding memory is the spirit of good fellowship in our tour party. I didn't hear one cross word pass between any of the players from October till mid April, and I wonder how many touring parties can say that?

It was the first time I'd been abroad and my eyes were opened on the month-long sea journey. I saw Gibraltar, Marseilles, Naples, Port Said, Suez and Ceylon. We once went ten days in the Indian Ocean when the only sign of human life was the sailing clippers on their way to England.

That month was a great experience because we had time to build up that fine team spirit that lasted throughout the tour. And I spent many happy hours talking cricket with players of great knowledge. Only one man didn't enjoy the boat trip. Jack Hobbs was always a poor sailor; if ever there was a slight swell he'd take to his deckchair, so he was allowed to journey by road to Marseilles where the boat picked him up, thereby avoiding the dreaded Bay of Biscay.

We were well paid for the honour of playing in Australia. I got £300 plus 30/– a week spending money. There was no such thing as a good conduct or a crowd bonus, and we had to buy our own equipment out of the £300. We were each given a tour blazer and a sash but no sweater—you could wear any type you liked.

I often smile to myself when I hear about touring parties taking physiotherapists with them and all the modern training paraphernalia. We didn't have a physio with us, we had just a baggageman. We kept ourselves fit, didn't do all this physical jerks stuff, but just did simple breathing exercises. And the only man to miss out was the captain, Plum Warner—and that was through a duodenal ulcer. It had nothing to do with our lack of a physio.

Looking back on it now, I suppose it was a stroke of good fortune for me that Warner was taken ill after the first match. I was well aware that he thought highly of Herbert Strudwick and I had no doubts that he'd keep in the Tests. But the replacement captain, Johnny Douglas, was a different type: where Warner always wanted the pros to look up to him and to let them realize he was the boss, Johnny was as straight as a gunbarrel. There was none of this 'Mr Douglas' nonsense with him. He let you know where you stood with him. He was one of us, more of a professional amateur than an amateur of the old school. We all respected him greatly for his strong qualities, and his honesty and the success of that tour owed a lot to Johnny Douglas.

It was Johnny who decided I'd play in the second Test because Strudwick had been given his chance in the first Test and he wanted to be fair to us both. My subsequent success never harmed my relationship with Struddy; at all times he was a perfect gentleman, he never put a straw in my way, and at all times he was modest and pleasant.

Our different attitudes towards keeping were obvious right at the start of the tour. We were in the nets at Adelaide before the first match and Warner spotted I wasn't keeping in the nets. 'I see Struddy's in the nets,' he said. 'The best keeper will play in the Tests, you know,' he said. Well that didn't bother me because I had my own system. I always kept a lacrosse ball in my pocket and for ten minutes every morning I'd throw it against the wall and try to take it. It was quicker than the ordinary cricket ball, came off the wall sharply and definitely helped my reactions throughout my career.

Struddy thought it was okay to practise in the orthodox manner behind the stumps in the nets, but I didn't agree. You're restricted in your movements in the nets, particularly on the leg side. Another practising technique I used on that tour: I'd get a stump in the ground and ask Jack Hobbs, Jimmy Iremonger, Joe Vine and Sep Kinneir to throw at me from different angles in a wide circle. That way I adjusted to the extra bounce of Australian wickets and kept myself sharp by running around to take the returns.

But the crucial difference was the way I took Frank Foster. I was lucky because I was used to my county captain's line and his surprising lift off the pitch, and with the Australian pitches so hard it was clear he'd be a handful for the Aussie batsmen. Foster made no secret of the fact that he thought I took him better than Struddy and once Foster and I had worked out a plan to keep the Aussie left-handers quiet it must have been obvious that I should stay in the Test side.

Vernon Ransford, Clem Hill and Warren Bardsley were the three left-handers, and fine, dangerous players they were. If we were to have any hope in the series it was vital to stop these three scoring heavily. So we decided to get them playing outside the leg stump, hope they over-balanced, and try for some leg-side stumpings. The margin of error was very small, though; if we bowled on their middle and leg, they'd work us away in typical Australian style.

In the second match I played, against Queensland, I showed I could carry out my part of the plan. I stumped Fett down the leg side off Syd Barnes, and I know Plum Warner was impressed with that. So all I could do now was wait for my chance in a Test match.

In that first Test at Sydney we were well beaten by 146 runs, thanks to some fine leg-break bowling by H. V. Hordern. He took 12 wickets in the match and none of our boys played him well. I watched all of the play and I can still see some of the lovely late-cutting and straight-driving of Victor Trumper, who made 113.

Clem Hill didn't open with Victor. He put him in number 5 because he thought he took a dart at the bowling too early in his innings. He batted just under four hours for his century yet Plum Warner wrote 'at no time did he let himself go'—today any Test batsman would be quite happy with a four-hour century. Warner also wrote that 'Australia had to fight for their runs'—yet at the end of the first day they'd made 315 for 5 in five hours!

Hordern was an interesting googly bowler. He gave the ball a lot of air and, like Sonny Ramadhin, he had the ability to make the ball hustle straight through on occasions. Well he certainly had us in knots at Sydney but the irrepressible George Gunn prophesied 'I'll put the ironclad on him'— and he did.

After losing the first Test, we were completely written off by the Press and the Australian public. We were too old, our young players weren't good enough, Hobbs had lost his touch, and the captaincy of Douglas wasn't a patch on Warner's. Some bookies offered odds of 5:1 against England winning a Test and Billy Hitch for one was delighted to put some money on that one, and clean up within a fortnight.

So to Melbourne and my first Test. I'd been told on Christmas Day I'd be in, and looking back on it now, all I can remember thinking was that I'd do my best. The team spirit was so good that I knew we'd fare better than at Sydney. I slept like a log the night before after having a couple of beers and I got to the ground nice and early. And what an introduction it was to Test cricket!

That first morning will always be remembered as Syd Barnes's morning. At one stage he'd taken 4 for 6 and the Aussies were 38 for 6! Yet it could so easily have been different if I hadn't thrown the ball to Barney at the end of the first over from Foster. You see, Johnny Douglas had opened the bowling with Foster at Sydney and the disgruntled Barney was heard to say, 'I can bowl with the new ball as well, you know.' I hadn't remembered that when I threw the ball to Barney for the start of the second over. It was just a natural thing on my part.

Well, Barney needed no second bidding and he was off to the railway end like a shot to pace out his run up. Johnny Douglas joined him swiftly and after a long chat, Barney got his way and the rest is history.

His first ball was to Warren Bardsley. It was on leg and middle and he tried to turn it round to leg. He was late on the shot and it trickled between his legs on to the wicket. Australia 0 for 1. In walks the captain, Clem Hill, to face a torrid over. The first ball's an lbw appeal from Barney that's turned down because it was going down the leg-side—a good decision. The next 4 balls are on the stumps and it needs all Hill's technique to keep them out.

But he didn't survive for long. Barney bowled him through the gate with a beautiful slower ball. I can still see that one now—Clem played forward and it hit the top of the middle and off stumps. Australia 5 for 2.

Charlie Kelleway didn't last long. Barney bowled him a quicker one, he played back, it came into him and he was plumb lbw. Australia 8 for 3 and Barney's saying 'I told you so' to Johnny Douglas.

Then Warwick Armstrong gave me my first catch in Test cricket. It was Barney's quicker one on the offside. He tried to cut it and I caught him up by my right shoulder. I was elated and after 45 minutes Australia were 11 for 4 and Barney had taken 4 for 0. The first runs off him were a snick through Douglas's legs at slip by Victor Trumper and at lunch they were 32 for 4.

The wicket was a beauty and none of the Aussie batsmen offered any excuse. It was simply a fine piece of brainy bowling by a great bowler. His length was immaculate and he didn't use any outfield even for Trumper and Armstrong. Throughout that morning, he bowled with three slips, a point, fine leg, midwicket, a mid-on, mid-off and cover point. And if ever there was a man who bowled to his field it was Barney.

We weren't done with sensations for that day, though. After lunch Barney got another quick wicket to give him 5 for 6 and Australia, with Foster taking a wicket, were 38 for 6. Then the trouble started and it was caused by the worst umpiring display I'd ever seen. George Gunn caught Hordern at slip and I picked up Sam Carter—both off Barney—and on each occasion Elder, the umpire, gave them not-out. We couldn't believe it. Barney called Elder a cheat and folded his arms and refused to bowl and the crowd went mad. We were furious but eventually Barney continued and he finished with 5 for 44. The Aussies rallied to 184 but our master bowler had won the Test for us on that first, famous day.

The feature of England's modest 265 was a lovely hundred from Jack Hearne, made before he reached 21 years of age. I was delighted for him because we palled up on the tour.

Then in the Australian second innings I fell foul of Warwick Armstrong. He was a big ordeal even then and already starting to throw his weight about and I knew he'd backed himself to score a century against us in the series. When Foster yorked him for 90 I chortled, 'You haven't got your hundred yet then Warwick'—and he swished his bat angrily, glared at me and stalked off.

Frank Foster was the hero this time, taking 6 for 91, and I got a leg-side stumping off his bowling, this time the left-hander Vernon Ransford. The Aussie batsmen just weren't used to Foster's pace off his short run, they made the mistake of playing back on a hard wicket, so he'd be through them before they could play a shot. So they got more defensive, which led to catches in the slips and at the wicket. And we'd already put the Indian sign on the three left-handers—they only made 97 in six innings in the match.

Our fielding was superb—George Gunn caught Clem Hill in the slips as easily as taking a plum off a tree and Jack Hobbs ran Warren Bardsley out with an underarm flick. He was so far out I could've dropped it, picked it up and still ran him out.

So we had only 219 to make and in their first Test match

together as an opening pair, Jack Hobbs and Wilfred Rhodes put on 57, and they looked as if they'd been batting with each other for years. They were to cause the Aussies a few headaches before the end of the tour. Hobbs got a beautiful unbeaten hundred and he and George Gunn kept walking up the wicket to Hordern and playing him easily away. We'd laid the Hordern bogey, won by eight wickets, and the bookies were left to wail and gnash their teeth.

I kept my place for the next Test at Adelaide, so Foster and I had another chance to put our leg-side plan into action. We couldn't wait to get at Clem Hill. In the first Test I'd noticed he overbalanced when Frank Woolley bowled to him, and at close quarters at Melbourne he was doing the same to Foster. We were so confident we could outwit Clem that I told Warner before the third Test that he'd be out, stumped Smith bowled Foster.

When Clem walked in, I told Foster to send one down the leg side any time he liked. The first ball was 18 inches down the leg side and he didn't play it. The second was about a foot wide. He tried to run it past square-leg's left hand off the front foot. He overbalanced and I had the bails off sharpish. The square-leg umpire Bob Crockett said, 'Good God, Clem, you're out,' and I replied, 'Ay, and a long way.' We were thrilled because one of the greatest pleasures in cricket is to set a trap for a fine player and to see him fall to it.

And Clem should've bagged 'em in that match. I stumped him again off Foster in the second innings before he'd scored yet umpire Watson gave him not out. I swear he was as far out as in the first innings yet he survived. If Bob Crockett, a fine brave umpire, had been at square leg, Clem would've bagged 'em.

But my biggest thrill at Adelaide came after the Test had finished. Blackham, the great Australian wicketkeeper of the 'eighties and 'nineties, came up to me and said, 'Well kept, young 'un', and praised my stumping of Clem. That meant more to me than any of the newspaper praise because Blackham was truly one of the greats.

That Adelaide Test is so vivid in my memory still. I can remember almost every ball. Hobbs and Rhodes put on 147 for the first wicket and made it look so easy. They picked on particular fielders and exposed their slowness or their poor returns. Clem Hill tried to frustrate Jack by placing a man deep to block his square-drive and square-cut. But Jack didn't trouble—he kept placing his shots down to that fielder and running an easy two. Jack was dropped five times after reaching his hundred but he always had a go after getting to the century and his 187 was a delight.

I didn't bat badly either. I made only 22 but I hit a screamer along the ground past Hordern, the bowler. I hit it on the half-volley and it rebounded halfway back into the field from the fence. I got carried away then, straight-drove Tibby Cotter (and he was fast) only to see my team mate Joe Vine, fielding as sub, take a lovely running catch. I said 'Why the hell didn't you drop it Joe?' but he was too fair a man for that.

I'll never forget the heat at Adelaide. On the second day it was 99 in the shade and 153 in the full glare of the sun. When I kept in that match the glare kept bouncing off the pitch and I felt as if the ground was coming up to meet me as I crouched down. I had a bad headache and put some green baize under my cap and a silk scarf round my neck to keep the sun away.

I was pleased with my first-innings catch of Bardsley. He snicked Barney between his leg and the wicket, I saw it early and took the inside edge standing up. Even Barney was moved to say, 'Well held, Tiger.'

So we ran out easy winners by seven wickets, and the Aussies were beginning to look a demoralized team. The crowds were very generous to us, but the Press hadn't warmed to us yet. They thought we were stodgy and unexciting. Mind you, that was sour grapes because I've never seen an Australian side go into a Test and try to hit the ball out of sight right from the start. We were playing it the Australian way—hard but fair—and we were trying to win as comprehensively as possible. I think that 5:1 bet was still rankling a few Australians who'd lost too much money. . . .

We won the fourth Test at Melbourne even more convincingly, by an innings. The Aussies were having a lot of behind-the-scenes wrangling. Clem Hill punched Peter McAlister, the chairman of the selectors, on the nose at one meeting and several of the players were demanding that Frank Laver should manage the side to England later that year. They were a demoralized side and once Foster and Barnes got them out for 191 on the first day, they were in trouble.

We then saw a magnificent stand of 323 for the first wicket by Hobbs and Rhodes. I was privileged to watch one of the most famous opening stands in Test history and believe me, it was an education. I learned more about the art of run-getting that day than ever before or since. Their command was effortless—Jack all graceful strokes and calmness, Wilfred, stiff-legged and sensible, working the ball away to his heart's content.

Their running between the wickets was a joy. They avoided the fine fielders like Trumper and Ransford and picked out poor Hordern. They kept playing the ball to his left hand at point and running singles. Once either moved, they were off—no 'yes' or 'no' was needed.

And yet the Australian press criticized them for slow scoring. One paper described Jack's innings as 'slow and methodical', yet he reached his century in 143 minutes. Wilfred only took $3\frac{1}{2}$ hours to reach his ton and the *Melbourne Age* cricket-writer moaned, 'To call it playing a game is a misuse of words. They never smiled nor took risks.' What did they expect? It was a Test match, not a game of ludo. . . .

The crowd took it well, though at one stage a wag shouted, 'If you don't get them out, we'll shoot them.'

When I went in at number ten the score was 579 and Plum Warner had asked me to stay in so we could pass the record score—587 by Australia. He desperately wanted to beat the record and even though I've never given records a thought,

I was glad to oblige with the record-breaking shot when I clipped Jim Matthews for two past mid-on. We were all out for 589 and the Aussies collapsed for 173 in the second knock.

I was surprised they folded up so meekly but it was clear the off-field rows were bothering them. Victor took 80 minutes to score 28 and Clem 50 minutes for 11 and they just couldn't get our bowlers away.

There was an interesting end to the match that must seem odd to today's cricket fans. England needed to take just one more wicket with Hordern and Ransford holding out when they went off for tea! In those days, the Laws decreed that the tea interval was taken at the arranged time. There was no flexibility. So while the crowd jeered the umpires, we sat sipping our cuppas waiting to go out and capture the final wicket to give us back the Ashes.

So to the last Test at Sydney, which we won by 70 runs. Before a ball was bowled something amazing happened. The Australian captain, Clem Hill didn't know who was in his side! The rows between him and the selectors were so prolonged now that they wouldn't tell him the make-up of his team. When Johnny Douglas was told this he sent Clem off with the words, 'Tell your selectors we don't toss up till I know your eleven.' I've never known such an incident in my career and Clem showed what he thought of the whole affair by fielding in the deep throughout the match—an odd place to find a skipper.

Clem had told me some of his problems in the previous Test. Then he'd wanted Charlie Macartney in the team, he wired Peter McAlister 'Suggest play Macartney.' The chairman wired back 'Suggest play Macartney and drop yourself.' Well that was no way to talk to a man of such experience and skill and Hill went for McAlister at a meeting. When McAlister came out, he didn't look so pretty.

In the end Hill, Armstrong, Carter, Ransford, Cotter and Trumper didn't go to England for the Triangular Tournament because they disapproved of the manager. A lot of bad blood was spilt and it only proves that the Australian players had problems with their Board of Control long before Kerry Packer came along to capitalize on it.

So it was Victor's last Test and each time he was dismissed the same way—caught Woolley, bowled Barnes. Woolley also scored a typically powerful hundred and during that innings he was a couple of inches away from killing little Syd Gregory. Frank hit a screamer at Syd, who was standing at cover point, and it went so hard it knocked Syd's cap off before he could get a hand to it. Woolley's driving that day was magnificent—I can still see Hordern bowling and skipping out of the firing line towards mid-off.

Warwick Armstrong made a tactical blunder on the fourth day. They were 191 for 3 needing 362 when Armstrong appealed against the light at about four o'clock. I couldn't understand his thinking because our bowlers were tired after a long, hard tour and the light wasn't all that bad. Well, it rained for two days after that, but all Tests were timeless ones in Australia in those days, so the time factor wasn't important. But the rain turned the wicket into a real 'sticky' and Australia never had a chance when play re-started. Foster and Barnes took eight wickets between them and it was a procession. Jack Hobbs ran Bardsley out again, giving him fifteen run-outs on the tour, and I was hit in the throat when a half-volley leapt up. But I was raised on rice puddings and dumplings, not the custard they give you nowadays, and I wouldn't go off. . . .

In his book of the tour Plum Warner thought I didn't keep very well in this final Test because I let too many byes through. I let 36 through in the match but all the time I was trying for stumpings and catches. Several times the ball passed between my gloves and the leg stump because I anticipated that the batsman might turn the ball into my hands, and on the last day the wicket was dodgy. No, I was quite happy with my form in that match.

I was happy with my form on the tour. I kept wicket as well as I was allowed to and yet I was only really pleased about one dismissal—my stumping of Clem Hill at Adelaide because I'd worked for that one. My other dismissals were all fairly straightforward and I can honestly say I didn't drop anything—they all fell out!

My batting wasn't so hot, only 139 runs on the tour—but at least I didn't tire myself out with the bat. I was always under instructions to get quick runs, something I've always liked to do anyway, and most of the time I got myself out.

I still have so many memories of that tour. Take the train journeys. It would take 14 hours to get from Adelaide to Melbourne, 16 hours from Melbourne to Sydney and from Sydney to Brisbane—29 hours. And we had to travel by night to avoid the heat. Even then it was devilish hot.

We were all friends together in the party. Never a jealous word passed between any of us and Johnny Douglas deserves all the credit for being such a fine leader. He'd never play the heavy-handed one; he'd let you know well in advance whether you were playing in the next match. If you weren't, he'd say, 'I want you with us for the match after. I don't care where you go or what you do but I want you back, fit and ready for cricket.' He treated us like men and we responded to that. I got on tremendously with Johnny—he took me shooting and fishing for a week in Tasmania halfway through the tour. Imagine it, Tiger Smith from the backstreets of Birmingham hob-nobbing with an amateur educated at Felsted College! But there was no 'side' to Johnny; he was as straight as they come. It was typical of the man that he should die in the Kattegat trying to save his father when he himself could have survived. He was that sort of man.

And how he loved to battle on the cricket field. Against Victoria at Melbourne, he batted for five and a half hours for 140, and I can see him now, capless (God knows how he could do that in such heat), pulling his gloves on with his teeth, saying to me at the other end, 'Stay there, Tiger, stay there.' A local newspaper pointed out that more trains passed the ground than he scored runs in an hour, and the

Press boys christened him 'Johnny Won't Hit Today' at the end of the tour. . . .

Only one criticism of Johnny Douglas from me. I think he could've given Jimmy Iremonger a game in the last Test. After all, we'd won the Ashes. Jimmy was the only man apart from Warner not to play in a Test and he wouldn't have let the side down because he nearly did the 'double' for Nottinghamshire in 1911. But the selectors obviously wanted to beat their opponents out of sight and even though Jimmy was terribly homesick throughout the tour, they didn't feel sorry for him.

I'm often asked if I stood back to anybody on that tour. I did to Billy Hitch on occasions because he could be erratic, and when Frank Foster bowled I'd have a couple of sighters before standing up to him. Apart from that I stood up to everyone. My opposite number on the Australian side stood back to Tibby Cotter and MacLaren in the final Test but no-one else. Sam Carter used to walk a couple of paces towards the stumps as the bowler took his final leap. I think Sam felt those two paces steadied him. He was a fine keeper— neat, unhurried and fair. In our 589 at Melbourne, Sam allowed only two byes.

And what was Syd Barnes's speed on that tour, they ask? Well, he was medium to slow, faster than men like D'Oliveira or Underwood. He really used his six-feet-two to make the ball get up when he wanted. If he had a stock ball, it was one just short of a length, pitching ten feet from the stumps, putting the batsman in 'no-man's land'. If you played back to Barney, you had to get into the proper position because his height made it hurry through. Both Barney and Foster so demoralized the Aussies that they kept playing back on hard, fast wickets, and that often proved fatal.

Eighteen of Foster's 32 victims in the Tests were bowled. He was so aggressive and so accurate that the Aussies never mastered his leg-side attack. He was the ideal foil for Barney. The older man was cunning and resourceful and Frank was hostile and could bowl all day.

So we sailed home triumphant. No side from England had ever won four Tests in Australia and we were sure we'd put the doubting Thomases in their place. It was the finest side I'd played in and the happiest. At the age of 26, I already had enough memories to last me a lifetime. . . .

5

THE TRIANGULAR TOURNAMENT

We arrived back from Australia in April. We had to come overland from Marseilles otherwise the boat would've taken too long to get to England and we would've missed the start of the season. That overland trip had other compensations because it meant we could spend a night in Paris. . . .

Within three weeks I was playing in a Test Trial. I suppose it must have looked a certainty that I'd keep in the forthcoming Triangular Tournament involving ourselves, Australia and South Africa, but I honestly didn't see it that way. When you're brought up with the seat of your pants hanging out, you learn to take nothing for granted and although I'd had a good tour, I knew there were many experienced keepers around. I always thought Joe Murrell of Middlesex a better keeper than me—the Lord's wicket in those days was a really fiery one and season in, season out, Joe did very well.

I kept in both Test Trials and the Smith/Foster combination worked again; we got Philip Mead out three times and I know Plum Warner was impressed because I told him how Mead would be out at Lord's. I must have fared well because I was retained in the England team for a summer that was an anti-climax for players and public.

The Triangular Tournament was a good idea in principle, but for such a competition to work you've got to have fine weather and evenly matched sides. The World Cup in 1975 was a great success for those reasons but in 1912 it was a disaster. For a start the weather was terrible, it seemed to rain all that summer and I remember in the Test Trial I was never so glad to get off a cricket field. Having just arrived back from Australia I wasn't acclimatized to the cold and the wind seemed to get into every part of my body. So if we England players felt the cold, what about our visitors?

England were just too strong for the other two. The Australian side had been ripped open by their feuds and most of their best players stayed at home. Syd Gregory, a very nice individual, captained the side but he was over the hill as a player and he captained the team as well as he was allowed to by the other players. They didn't pull together in the usual Australian manner and it was clear that some of them were only there for the trip. They were easily the worst Australian team to visit England—far worse than the 1956 and 1977 sides—they were no match for an England XI which was one of the strongest of its time. The fact that only half of the successful side that went to Australia could get into our team in 1912 shows how strong we were.

The South Africans were very weak as well. Their best batsman, Herby Taylor, had his best days ahead of him and although great old scouts like Frank Mitchell and Dave Nourse tried hard, they weren't up to it. They were a great side to play against, though. Unlike the dour Australians, they had some real live-wires in their party and there was never a dull moment with them. But the public didn't want to know about things like that. They wanted keen, competitive cricket. But too many of the tournament games were over in two days or washed out.

In our first Test at Lord's against South Africa we saw the shape of things to come. Barnes and Foster took 19 wickets between them, Foster hit the stumps five times, they were all out for 58, and Jack Hobbs was put on to bowl seam-up to prolong the game on the third day. Among those playing for England who didn't go to Australia were Reggie Spooner, C. B. Fry, Walter Brearley and Gilbert Jessop—that shows the all-round strength of English cricket at that time.

Our first match against Australia was memorable for a brilliant 99 from Charlie Macartney. He batted only 140 minutes and he pulled Barney for a tremendous six, but then I caught him down the leg side off Frank Foster. It was easy as anything—he just followed the ball and placed it straight into my hands. Afterwards Charlie told me he was on a £100 bonus if he'd got his century, a lot of money in those days.

Charlie Kelleway hung on for over 4½ hours for 61 and bored the pants off everyone. He still hadn't learned his lesson from the games in Australia where Barnes and Foster eased up and were happy to keep him in. If Charlie stayed in, the batsman at the other end would often get frustrated because the scoring was so slow and he'd get out. So while Charlie kept an end up he was no danger to us.

Jack Hobbs got a fine century in this match on a tricky, rain-soaked wicket. That's why Jack's always been the tops in my book, he could get runs on any wicket at any time. Considering he suffered badly from migraine throughout his life, his career was magnificent. Many a time Jack would turn to me at the crease and ask if I had any pills for a headache but he never let people know how much he suffered.

The Old Trafford match against Australia was, not surprisingly, washed out. There was just time for Wilfred Rhodes to get 92 in the mud and he played with all his usual dogged determination. A great self-made batsman was Wilfred. Like a true Yorkshireman he never gave his wicket away.

I picked up six stitches in a split lip against the South Africans at The Oval. Barney bowled a leg-break fairly wide, Herby Taylor followed it round and the bat and ball hit me in the mouth at the same time. Kept me quiet for a bit, but I was back behind the stumps after lunch.

The only real game was the Australian Test at The Oval. It was to be played to a finish but our left-arm spinners Frank Woolley and Harry Dean finished them off. C. B. Fry played one of the finest innings I've ever seen. He made 79 on a difficult wicket with some magnificent driving against Gerry Hazlitt, who bowled medium-pace off-spin, took 7 for 25 and had all the rest of us in a terrible state.

When Fry's great innings ended, I was next man in. 'Stay there for as long as possible,' he ordered me as I passed him. I took a couple of balls, realized that if Fry had the skill to stay there I hadn't, took a swipe and was bowled by Hazlitt. Barney was next in and I said 'You don't want to stay there very long.' 'Why?' he said. 'You'll see when you get out there.' And he did—the ball was turning square, but C. B. Fry hadn't realized it because he was playing so well. He didn't appreciate that ordinary mortals wouldn't last on that pitch and he gave me, Harry Dean and Barney—who all got ducks—the bird for throwing our wickets away.

But we knew what we were doing. We wanted a couple of hours at them that night and we wanted Macartney and Bardsley out. Warren was run out by Jack Hobbs for a duck and Harry Dean and I schemed out Charlie.

Harry was bowling from the pavilion end and Macartney was cutting him easily down to the Vauxhall end. I said to Harry, 'Can you make one go with your arm?' 'Yes.' 'Well it's about time you did—he's cutting your spinner too easily.' Third ball next over. Harry made it go with his arm and he knocked Charlie's leg peg down.

We got them all out for 65 that night and proved to C. B. Fry that the pros knew something about the game. But all he said was, 'I didn't think the wicket was turning that way.'

Although the Triangular Tournament was a failure I was happy with my own form. I still wasn't scoring many runs for England but my main job was to keep wicket and I just did that in my own natural way. I've never been a nervous person and I've always maintained that the better the bowler, the easier the job is for the keeper. And England had a great attack at that time; it was a pleasure to keep to them all.

The 1912 season was an anti-climax for Warwickshire as well. We slipped from first to ninth in the table and the decline in Frank Foster's form was the main reason. He was tired after his exertions of the last year and he got carried away with bowling too much leg theory. He'd seen Roy

Minnett try it at Melbourne and he shifted his line from leg and middle to leg and just outside. But that took the element of surprise away from his bowling and with the wickets lacking bounce because of the wet summer, he wasn't so devastating. I tried to get him to change his line but he just laughed. Success had come quickly to Frank and he couldn't be bothered thinking too much about his game.

Still I was happy and contented. Little did I realize I only had one more England cap to win. . . .

6
SOUTH AFRICA 1913/14

I wasn't originally selected for the South African tour, partly because Frank Foster couldn't go for business reasons and also because Lord's wanted to send some amateurs out to get some sunshine. We all knew we could send out any side and beat the South Africans because we were so strong at the time, so among the amateurs sent were Lionel Tennyson, M. C. Bird and the Gloucestershire wicket-keeper D. C. Robinson.

Now I suppose it must seem strange to you that England's number one keeper from the previous season shouldn't be picked. Well there was nothing wrong with my form in 1913—I scored nearly 1000 runs and snapped up 66 victims, the largest haul in my career. But the amateurs still ruled the roost and it was a custom for them to go to South Africa.

I didn't see the point in grumbling. I was happy with my form and I wasn't to know world war was just round the corner and that my England career was nearly over. Besides, Lord's had put me on standby in case D. C. Robinson's health gave out. Sure enough when I got back from a holiday in Blackpool with the wife at the end of October a cable was waiting for me. 'Proceed to Lord's immediately' it said and I was off like a shot.

It took three weeks by boat and I joined the side at East London. Johnny Douglas was the skipper and I'm sure my selection had a lot to do with him. No doubt Lord's insisted on the other amateurs but Johnny was always honest with me and I know he was delighted to have me and Herbert Strudwick in his squad again. D. C. Robinson didn't play a match . . .

I suppose to the modern cricket world a lot of strange things happened on that tour—and I don't just mean Tiger Smith playing in a Test for his batting and fielding at mid-on! For a start we didn't have our own manager from England. Ivor Difford was supplied by the South African Cricket Association and so was our baggageman, who acted as pavilion attendant. We didn't even bring a scorer out with us. And there were only 13 players in the party, compared with 16 in Australia two years earlier.

Because they knew we'd win, MCC didn't bother too much about the tour and the South African Cricket Association had to pay our expenses and tour fees of £200. And the Association didn't have much spare cash so they could only afford to finance 13 England players.

The players weren't happy with Ivor Difford as manager. At Johannesburg a lot of rumours started flying around that we were a team of boozers. This was because Ivor and the baggageman collected the half-empty bottles of beer, wine and spirits left for the players to drink after the day's play. Most of us had just a swig and we assumed the rest would go back to the club that donated them. But he and his side-kick hung on to them and took them away in the skip without our knowledge.

So one or two Press stories suggested we liked our drink, which was ridiculous considering who was on the tour. Jack Hobbs, Johnny Douglas, Wilfred Rhodes, Frank Woolley and Phil Mead hardly ever touched a drop, a tot or two of scotch was enough for Bert Relf, Struddy used to drink ginger beer at dinners and other functions, Barney didn't drink much, and the only ones who really liked a glass of beer were myself, Jack Hearne and Lionel Tennyson.

We were annoyed that some of our splendid South African hosts had got the wrong idea but that was nothing compared to the ructions in the team when we were due to sail home. Ivor Difford tried to deduct money from some of the players—he tried to take £50 off me because I hadn't played on the full tour, Bert Relf was £10 short, Phil Mead a fiver and Jack Hearne was short because he'd been in hospital at Durban and the manager thought Jack should pay for that!

There was a hell of a rumpus. Johnny Douglas argued with Difford, made sure I got my £200 and all the other lads got their full whack as well.

I must say there were a few misunderstandings on that tour—like the time we supposedly snubbed the Mayor of Bloemfontein. It was in the heart of the Boer country and memories were still fresh of the bitter struggle between the British and the Boers. Anyway we turned up on the train to play a match without realizing that we were supposed to have been greeted at the station by the Mayor. No-one told us and we left by another entrance and made our way to the hotel.

So the Mayor was left standing at the station with the red carpet and he and his supporters took it as a political snub. The local Press had a field day and the civic dignitaries cancelled a trip for us to the Boer War battlefield the next day. Luckily Barney and Rhodes decided we weren't going to hang around there too long. They bowled the opposition out twice in a day and we left in a hurry.

Then there was the time we played at Benoni. A general strike was on and martial law had been declared. We needed special passes to move around at night and we played in front of not one single spectator. Gatherings were forbidden by martial law and it was an eerie experience, I can tell you.

But despite the problems with the manager and the other misunderstandings we all enjoyed the tour. I'd been out there the previous winter coaching—I did this for many years—and I liked the climate and the people. Unfortunately the cricket was a little one-sided but I decided to enjoy myself in this lovely country as soon as I joined the team and heard some of them say that they felt sorry for Strudwick because they thought I was going to squeeze him out of the Test side again. Now Struddy's always been a perfect gentleman to me and remembering how sporting he was to me in Australia even though he must've been disappointed,

51

I was determined not to stand in his way. So I relaxed, didn't trouble about taking the gloves and enjoyed watching the others working in the Tests!

I played in nine games but only kept in five of them. I played in one Test, the second at Johannesburg. I batted number nine and fielded mid-on. I never cared for fielding throughout my career and yet here was I, in only my second first-class game as a fielder, at mid-on in a Test! I took one catch—if it'd been a hard one I'd have dropped it—and it gave Wilfred Rhodes his 100th Test wicket. It was a dolly from Gerry Hartigan who'd made 51 at the time.

In that Test, Barney took 17 wickets. It was a magnificent display, particularly in the second innings, when he took 9 for 103. Time after time he beat the bat and the extra bounce from the matting took the ball just over the stumps. He was well-nigh unplayable and I consider it a finer piece of bowling than his famous 4 for 6 spell at Melbourne in my first Test.

Barney simply demoralized the South Africans. The matting wickets had a tendency to lift and take spin and I lost count of the times he was too good for the rabbits who couldn't put a bat to him. It was the finest bowling I've seen anywhere, even though the opposition was so poor. He bowled at the same pace as in Australia but he got tremendous lift on the matting.

I remember a fascinating struggle between Barney and the South African opening pair, Billy Zulch and Herby Taylor. It was in the third Test and Barney was unbelievably unlucky. But Taylor and Zulch stuck to it and finally Barney had to take a rest after a magnificent spell of bowling. On comes Bert Relf and in his first over Billy Zulch is caught and bowled by him and then Herby hits a full toss down Lionel Tennyson's throat at long-on. All Barney could say was, 'I wish I could bowl a ball like that!'

Herby Taylor was the only one who could give Barney a battle. He was a great forward player, very patient and determined. Barney was always nicking the top of Herby's bat but he slackened the hands at the right time and the ball would drop short of a fielder. Barney was always trying for his outside edge but Herby's bat/pad play was a model.

Our team spirit was excellent on that tour—with a skipper like Johnny Douglas and characters like Lionel Tennyson it couldn't be anything else. I didn't feel professionally fulfilled because I knew Struddy's face fitted and I was pleased for him. But some of the matches shouldn't really have been ranked first-class and when you play cricket you want a good, hard but fair game. We returned to England in mid-April. Little did we realize that we were about to play our last full season till 1919.

7
THE POST-WAR PLAYING YEARS

Cricket was never quite the same after the Great War; the gaiety that the amateur batsmen brought to the game was gone for ever. The quality of bowlers was better in my opinion but crowds have always loved spectacular hitting and with the wickets getting easier there were too many high-scoring matches on featherbeds and too many mediocre players worried about their averages.

I was never as happy as a cricketer after the War. The rows with the committee and the secretary started and never really finished until I retired in 1930. The team was nowhere near as good as under Foster and there was a fair amount of back-biting from some of my fellow professionals at Warwickshire.

But at least I was in one piece after the War, thanks to a stupid sergeant-major. I'd enlisted in the Warwickshire Regiment and was on the parade ground at Sutton Coldfield getting barked at by the sergeant-major. We were marching at the double when he suddenly brought us to the halt. We were all so surprised we fell over—I ended up in the bottom of the scrum. I was laughing my head off until I realized I couldn't get up. My knee was swollen and after a few months I was discharged with cartilage trouble. I wasn't sorry—I saw many poor blokes coming back from the front with arms in slings and hobbling on crutches and yet people kept saying 'Oh, there's nothing like being a good soldier'.

I lost many cricketing friends in the War. Young Percy Jeeves was killed on the Somme, a tragedy because poor

Percy wasn't the fighting type. He was a lovely, gentle lad with a permanent smile on his face. I well remember his first match with us—against the Australians in 1912. Percy was on a fiver for his first wicket, and I got a fiver as well when I caught Kelleway off his bowling. He only played two full seasons for us but he was a fine all-rounder.

He was an 'arm' bowler and he hit the deck at fast–medium and could really hustle the batsman. His arm was low at the point of delivery and Yorkshire wouldn't take him on their books because of doubts over his action. But I never had any doubts about it and Warwickshire did very well to pluck him from village cricket.

Percy could really hit the ball. He was about 5ft. 7in. tall and his arms and body were together when he played the shot. I can see one of his biggest hits now—I was in the dressing-room and watched it soar clean out of the ground and land across the road. Percy would've been a great all-rounder for England if he'd lived.

We lost so many players in the war—Colin Blythe, K. L. Hutchings, Major Booth. And Victor Trumper also died of Bright's disease. I felt a terrible sense of waste. . . .

So we returned to the fray in 1919 to find that Lord's had been tampering with the rules again. Only two-day matches were to be played that year, and what a grind that was. The public weren't interested because the standard wasn't very good, there was hardly a decent finish and the players were exhausted. We often played till 7 o'clock and then you'd have to travel to, say, Manchester, change at Crewe and get there about midnight. Then it'd be off to Hull or London two nights later.

That season should've been one of transition. The County Championship should've been shelved or if there were to be two-day matches then it would've been just an innings each. By the end of that season I was tired out. Many of us were still weak from that terrible 'flu epidemic of late 1918 and I'd worked a seven-day week in a Birmingham munitions factory for the past four years.

My own form was up and down. It took several years to get attuned again to standing behind the stumps and I was never in with a chance of getting back into the England side for the matches against Australia in 1920 and 1921. But I did see that famous Australian opening pair of Gregory and McDonald when they came here in '21. They were the best pair of fast bowlers I've played against; I've seen better fast bowlers than either of them but as a pair they complemented each other so well.

'Mac' had a lovely flowing action from about 15 yards and because his run-up and delivery were so smooth, the speed of the ball always came as a shock. Gregory, on the other hand, would tear in like Bob Willis off a 20-yard run and hammer it in at you. He was over six feet tall so he made it rise sharply and was a more physically dangerous bowler than 'Mac'. But 'Mac' was by far the better bowler; he was an affable type, who liked a pint and a joke. When he played for Lancashire he formed a hard-drinking school with three others but because they were such good cricketers their skippers could never complain too much about them.

Although I didn't enjoy my cricket as much after 1914, I was lucky to have a very happy captain at Warwickshire. Freddie Calthorpe was a lovely fellow. He'd never let things get him down and encouraged us to play attacking cricket. He once lost the toss 13 times in a row but it didn't bother Freddie. A very shy man, if he saw you talking to someone he'd move away even if he wanted to tell you something. About 6ft. 2in. and as thin as a cabbage stalk, Freddie, unlike many amateurs, was worth his place in the side. He was a good medium-pace bowler and a fine attacking bat. I once saw him play a marvellous innings of 174 against Lancashire. Ted McDonald had his tail up but Freddie kept driving him away. That day 'Mac' hit him in the chest and he was never the same again. I saw him go blue a number of times on the field after that and he died in 1935 at the age of 43.

Bobby Wyatt, the man who succeeded Freddie as our skipper, was so different. Now Bobby was a fine player, a self-made one but he had a great defence, lots of guts and a record second to none among amateurs between the wars. But I didn't like his style of cricket. I thought he was an average-monger who played for himself too much whereas Freddie was always so delightfully unselfish. I've always respected Bobby Wyatt's cricket knowledge because he really thought about the game—he loved playing against Yorkshire because he said they played the game his way. I never like cricket that way—whenever I played Yorkshire it was 'good morning' and nothing else but 'howzat' for the rest of the day.

Bobby got a lucky break when he came to Edgbaston in 1923. Ryder took him on as assistant secretary so Bobby could play as an amateur. This meant he could practise for hours in the nets with the pros bowling at him while the pro batsmen could only have about 15 minutes each in the nets. So early on, Bobby got the chance to work at his game.

When he became skipper in 1930 I was senior pro and I told him 'I'll give you any advice you want, just ask for it, otherwise I'll say nothing.' He never asked for any, so I said nothing. He was a strong, dour man but I respected him in one way—he wouldn't take any nonsense from the committee and made it quite clear he wouldn't let them interfere in team matters. That's something dear old Freddie could never manage.

This interference by the committee and particularly by Ryder played a decisive part in one of the most famous matches of all time. The match was in 1922 at Edgbaston between Warwickshire and Hampshire when we bowled Hampshire out for 15 and still lost. I'm still embarrassed about it after all these years. . . .

We batted first on an easy-paced wicket and we were all out in mid-afternoon for 223. Hampshire started batting at four o'clock and 45 minutes later they were all out for 15—and don't ask me why. The wicket was well-nigh perfect although a bit quicker than the Hampshire boys had faced so far that season. One ball from Harry Howell flashed past me down the leg side and went for four byes before I could get up from my crouch but there was nothing wrong with the wicket. Howell bowled really fast that day—he took 6 for 7 and Freddie 4 for 4. At one stage they were 10 for 8 and we couldn't understand it on the field. So many of them were playing back instead of forward, yet they had some good players—Phil Mead, George Brown, Alec Kennedy, Alec Bowell, Lionel Tennyson. Only Phil Mead had any idea; he ended up six not out and never looked in any trouble.

It was ridiculous and to cap it all, Lionel Tennyson shouted out at the end of the innings, 'Never mind, lads, we'll get 500 next time.' By that time, the amateurs on either side were organizing games of golf for the next day. Only Lionel thought the game could be saved. He went round putting bets on with anyone who'd take them.

Then Freddie said to me 'Shall we make them follow on?' I said 'yes' like a shot and my advice would remain the same today. That night we got three more out, including Phil Mead, and Hampshire didn't have a hope. They reckoned without the influence of our committee and the guts of George Brown. . . .

Just before lunch on the second day, they'd lost six wickets and were still 30 behind. It was then that the committee took a hand; 'R.V.R.' sent a note to Freddie on the field saying that the committee wanted to see some cricket before they went into a meeting.

So Freddie delayed taking the new ball and gave occasional bowlers like Jack Smart, Reggie Santall, Jack Fox and Cyril Smart a bowl. At lunchtime I told the skipper, 'Get them out. Take no notice of Ryder.' But he continued with the change bowlers and poor Billy Quaife, who bowled 49 overs at the age of fifty!

When Freddie finally took the new ball, he and Harry Howell couldn't get George Brown out. He made 172, Walter Livsey made his first century batting at number 10, and they made 521, a lead of 313. We could only get 158, with Kennedy and Newman taking nine wickets, and we lost by 155 runs.

The result created a sensation in the Press and the players took a lot of stick from our supporters and, believe it or not, from the committee! Hampshire couldn't believe their luck and Lionel Tennyson scooped a lot of bets. A ridiculous match. . . .

But that wasn't the most amazing match I've played in. That was at Edgbaston in 1925 against Sussex. We needed 392 to win in four hours and we won by nine wickets with three-quarters of an hour to spare. I made 139 not out, the best innings I've ever played, Jack Parsons got 124 and Freddie Calthorpe 109 not out.

Jack and I opened and we had no instructions from Freddie. I took the first over from Maurice Tate. I got a juicy half-volley and drove it past Gilligan at cover for a boundary. We then started running singles to cover and mid-off to draw them in and then we'd drive over their heads. It was great fun against a fine fielding side.

I gave Jack a lot of the strike and he made his 124 out of 176 for the first wicket. When Freddie came in he said, 'Can you last out, Tiger?'—'Just watch me last out,' I said, and we tore into them. After we'd won, Freddie said, 'I think I owe you a drink, Tiger.' And we had a bottle of champagne together. I'd normally have to wait till 6 o'clock for a drink!

So many great games. There was the time in 1925 when we bowled Kent out for 42, with Calthorpe and Howell getting all the wickets. In their second knock, Kent had to get 342 to win. They won by seven wickets with Frank Woolley and Wally Hardinge getting centuries. That Hampshire result wasn't unique. . . .

I well remember my benefit match in 1922. I chose Lancashire because they were full of popular players. It rained all day on the Saturday and the Lancashire skipper, Miles Kenyon, went round on his own with a collection box. He wouldn't let anyone help him and I finally received £750—after I'd paid for the amateurs' fees, the professionals' wages, umpires' expenses, the teas and lunches and even a shilling cab fare to take the money to the bank!

There was the game at Huddersfield in 1922. It was a hard, bumpy wicket and the worst I've ever kept on. Jack Smart bust his thumb fielding at slip, Billy Quaife was hit in the ribs and we had to plaster him up, and everyone on our side bowled, including me. The slow-medium trundlers became holy terrors and it was all I could do to jump up and push a few over the bar. I stood up throughout the match, because if I'd stood back, the ball would've bounced right over my head. Percy Holmes got a double-hundred for Yorkshire and although he chanced his arm, it was a great knock on such a wicket.

Talking of Yorkshire, I can't forget the game at Hull when we ended their run of 70 unbeaten matches. Some of the Yorkshire boys took it badly and this was the game when Jack Parsons threatened George Macaulay. It was always nice to beat Yorkshire. . . .

I saw every ball of that famous Test at Edgbaston in 1924 when England dismissed South Africa for 30. Just as in that Hampshire match, I couldn't work out why class players were bowled out so cheaply. Gilligan (6 for 7) and Tate (4 for 12) couldn't be faulted but it was still a mystery to me. Gilligan's run—about 20 yards—made him look much faster than Maurice—about an eight-yard run—but there wasn't much to choose between them in pace. Maurice's right arm was so long that by the time he'd finished he was almost shaking hands with the batsman.

The England keeper was George Wood, the Kent amateur. I was still scratching around like an old hen behind the stumps and I never gave a thought to being picked for England again. It was the first time that Hobbs and Sutcliffe opened in a Test—and Herbert nearly ran Jack out in the first over. Herbert didn't realize that Jack just played the ball and ran, so Herbert was waiting for the call and sent Jack back. After that there were no misunderstandings and they became the best opening pair that I've seen. Hobbs and

Rhodes were just as good at stealing singles but Herbert was a better player than Wilfred, so that clinched it in my book.

This Test was Cecil Parkin's last. He was a temperamental character and he didn't take kindly to not getting a bowl for long periods. So he wrote an article in a newspaper saying he'd been badly treated by Gilligan and didn't want to play for him again. It was a silly thing to do because Parkin just wasn't fit to bowl; he had an injury to his arm and back and the Aston Villa trainer was summoned to massage him. His outburst in the Press was unprofessional and he didn't deserve to play for England again. He'd forgotten that the captain must ultimately be the sole judge of things on the field.

One man never forgot that Test. He was G. M. Parker, a South African then playing in the Bradford League. Herby Taylor persuaded him to play and he bowled 37 overs and took 6 for 152. But he wasn't used to running around all day and when he walked off the field at close of play he fainted.

Warwickshire's match against the South Africans was a lot of fun that year. That was the game when Len Bates lay down at third man for a quick kip. The game was drifting towards a draw and at the fall of a South African wicket, Len lay down for a spot of shut-eye but as soon as he realized we were trying to get the batsman to cut the ball down to him he got up! Freddie Calthorpe then put Len on to bowl, knowing how much he hated bowling. Much to Len's delight he had Blanckenberg caught in the deep by Norman Kilner. Len was a great character—he was the son of the old groundsman, Jack Bates, whom I worked under when I first started. Len was born on the ground and I never saw a more stylish bat play at Edgbaston. Jack Hobbs could never understand why he never made the England side— perhaps he was too easy-going.

Len always liked a laugh—in the early days of the war we were together at Sutton Coldfield. As usual Len had mis- behaved and was told to walk round the parade ground for two hours with a full rucksack. Instead of the 94-pound weight he put some balloons in and he strolled round. But when he put the rucksack on the floor, it bounced back up at him!

Once Len was asked to bowl against Middlesex. To show his disgust at such a waste of energy he bowled Nigel Haig a tremendous long-hop. It bounced twice, Nigel crouched down and flatbatted it straight back at Len. Len caught it and in the same instant fell flat on his back, laughing . . .

He even laughed when 'Doc' Gibbons of Worcester ran him out with a direct hit from the edge of the boundary at Edgbaston when Len had made 199. He was on the fourth run and he was out by half a yard.

I always had plenty of laughs when we played Glamorgan, particularly with Jack Mercer, who was a great joker. He fiddled me out when I'd made 97 against them in 1929. Jack said, 'I'll give you a four for your hundred down the leg side', but he gave me one that pitched middle and leg and had me lbw; I didn't mind, because that was Jack's way.

Another Glamorgan leg-puller was Dai Davies. He'd scored 99 and he said to young George Paine, 'Give us one for my hundred, youngster, and you can have my wicket then.' George obliged and Dai went on to get 150. . . .

Another happy match was the Gents v Players match at Folkestone in 1927. The festival games were always great fun and just to show we weren't taking it seriously, I was made the Players' captain—the only time I've captained a first-class side in my life. Jack Hobbs decided to liven up the afternoon play by slipping a bread roll into his pocket. He gave it to Jack Newman when his county captain, Lionel Tennyson, came in and I'll never forget Lionel's face when Newman bowled the roll at him!

I remember Warwickshire's match against West Indies in 1928 for a number of reasons. Jack Parsons hit the slow bowler O. C. Scott for four successive sixes and the next ball he was caught one-handed by Learie Constantine in front of the sightscreen. Then Learie knocked out Len

Bates. The ball hit Len in the throat, it went up in the air and their wicketkeeper, Karl Nunes, shouted 'Catch it!' I was in at the other end and I said, 'You don't play cricket that way, do you?' and Learie said, 'Sorry, Tiger.' It was just high spirits by the West Indians; they were a delightful side.

Later in the innings Learie gave a wonderful display of fielding. He picked up a ball at cover point, hit the wicket and while the appeal was being turned down, he bounded over to the other side and threw down the other wicket from mid-on. It was still 'not out' but it was out of this world.

Learie was so quick on his feet. When I toured West Indies in 1925–26 he ran in his bare feet to beat Len Crawley in a 100 yards race. And Len had won the Oxford and Cambridge 100 yards the previous year. As a fielder Learie was best when the ball came to him quickly. When he had to stop and think he wasn't as cool as Jessop or Hobbs and he gave away a lot of runs with wild throwing. But as a bowler he was as quick as anyone we have today. He wasn't much of a batsman although he was exciting to watch—he played cross-batted all the time and the best way to bowl at him was to throw it up and have the fielders deep. Learie would always accept the challenge.

That tour I had to West Indies was a marvellous one—even if I did catch malaria. Freddie Calthorpe was the skipper so it couldn't fail to be a happy party and I was the senior pro. We had some good players—Wally Hammond, Percy Holmes, Roy Kilner, Fred Root, Ewart Astill, Lionel Tennyson—and once I'd sorted out with the amateurs that the pros should be treated equally we got on fine.

Early in the tour the pros were having dinner at one table and the amateurs at the other. The manager, Major Levick, came over and said, 'Everything all right, boys' to which I replied, 'Well you've got a bottle of wine on your table and we haven't'—and every night after that we got a bottle of wine, paid for by the amateurs.

My room-mate on the tour was dear old Roy Kilner. We

went everywhere together; he was always laughing and joking. Two years later he died of typhoid after falling ill at Marseilles on the way back from coaching in India. I understand some of his last words were, 'This wouldn't have happened if Tiger was with me.' You see, I looked after Roy in the West Indies and told him to stay away from certain food and water. We cleaned our teeth in soda water and didn't eat everything put in front of us. But Roy was a happy-go-lucky soul and didn't take much care of himself in India. I lost a dear friend and his death hit me hard.

I thought I was on the way out at Georgetown when I caught malaria. It happened so simply; we were playing British Guiana and one of their men played Wally Hammond to cover. The non-striker, knew he wouldn't get in so he threw his bat. It hit me on the forehead and knocked me out. Two overs after I'd been carried off, Percy Holmes—who'd taken over the gloves—was carried back to the pavilion with a broken nose. So we both lay there in the pavilion, feeling sorry for ourselves and I suppose I was bitten by a mosquito there.

That night my temperature was 105. I heard the natives saying, 'White man gonna die, white man gonna die' and I thought my number was up. Freddie Calthorpe asked if I wanted anything. I asked for a whisky, plenty of hot water and the juice of four fresh limes. I was sweating so much you could've wrung me out. The next morning the doctor came in, looked surprised, and said, 'I thought you were ready for the box'—'I'm ready for a drink,' I said, so I knew I was much better.

Funnily enough I didn't miss any cricket; we didn't play again for another sixteen days but the effects stayed with me for years. Every November I'd get the fever, I'd shake like a leaf and take to my bed for a week.

I wasn't the only one to catch something on that tour. Wally Hammond caught the fever near the end of the trip and he went straight into hospital at Bristol when the ship docked. He missed the whole of the 1926 season, so the

Aussies didn't catch him until 1928–29. On that banana boat on the way back there weren't enough passengers on board to justify a ship's doctor, so we had to do the best we could and keep Wally warm and give him plenty of liquids.

Wally was grand company on that tour. I know many thought he was stand-offish later in his career but he took part in everything with us and loved a laugh. He was a great all-round games player and he showed his swimming skills at Kingston when he and I challenged Lionel Tennyson and Captain Jameson of Hampshire to a swimming race. Lionel was always one for some devilment so he decided to face Wally. I gave Wally a three-yard lead and and he just sped through the water in the pool. I don't think Lionel finished and Wally and I picked up a bottle of wine each.

Wally's batting made a deep impression on me in that tour. He and I put on over 120 in a match at Barbados and he made me look second-rate, even though I got over 70. His ease and power on the off side were magnificent and he scored a superb double-hundred. I shouted down the wicket to him, 'You make me look like a donkey, Wally' and he just laughed. But in 21 years of batting with the great players I'd never been outclassed like that and after that innings, I never took my batting seriously. I realized I wasn't in the same league as some players.

We had some great fun on that tour, particularly the time when Ewart Astill took the mickey out of Francis, the fast bowler. We were playing at Trinidad and a last-wicket stand was developing. A quick single was attempted and Francis was running to the bowler's end but he wasn't going to make it. Ewart stood over the bails with the ball in his hand, grinning at Francis, tempting him to dive. He did and when he got up his shirt, trousers, face and arms were red with the soil—and there was Ewart still standing over the stumps with the ball in his hand and still grinning his face off!

I actually got a wicket on that tour. It was the final game at Kingston and we couldn't get the tailenders out. I said to

Freddie, 'I could get this fellow out myself.' He let me take my pads off, I bowled a bloke called Bloomfield out third ball with an off-break and then at the end of the over Freddie said, 'Put your pads back on Tiger, I've seen enough.' So I finished top of the tour averages with one for none!

That wasn't the only wicket I took in first-class cricket. I got Patsy Hendren out at Lord's in 1920. He'd scored over a hundred and he hit an off-break pitched outside the off stump straight at Billy Quaife's chest. If Billy hadn't caught it, he'd have been killed. But I got him out and Patsy was top of the national averages that year. . . .

And I nearly got Jack Hearne once when he was on 97. It was a perfectly pitched off-break, it just missed his leg peg and he went on to get a double-hundred. Oh, I could turn the off-break, you know. . . .

Yes my bowling was just one of many laughs on my first and only trip to West Indies. I found the spectators delightfully enthusiastic and the players were honest and likeable. There were nine pros and six amateurs in the party and we all got on famously. On the trip back Freddie called me to his cabin. He opened a bottle of champagne and said, 'Tiger, I had to come on tour with you to really know you.' I was touched and it was a privilege to finish the bottle with him.

Freddie wasn't the only one I surprised on that tour. Ewart Astill confessed on the way back that before he thought I was 'a big brown bear'. Perhaps I'd appealed too loudly against him but after that trip we became great friends.

I came home to the 1926 season and the biggest disappointment of my life. Suddenly I was back with a chance of playing for England against the Australians that summer, when I'd never given a thought to playing for my country again.

The man who raised my hopes was the England captain, Arthur Carr, though I don't blame him for my eventual disappointment. Lord's still pulled the strings as he was to find out when he was dropped in favour of Percy Chapman for that final triumphant Test at The Oval.

It all started when I kept against Notts at Trent Bridge. The home skipper, Arthur Carr, told me at lunchtime that I'd keep for the North of England against the Australians. I didn't think much more about it until Fred Root bowled leg theory and 7 for 42. The Aussies didn't like it and Fred said, 'I wish you kept to me all the time.'

Ever since Frank Foster started in 1908, I've had no trouble on the legside and I can only assume Arthur Carr realized that. Why else would he want a man of 40 behind the stumps for England? Anyway I kept well to Geary and Larwood also in that match—it was the first time I'd taken Larwood; he was the quickest I've ever kept to and I had no hesitation in standing back to him.

Plum Warner was watching the match and he asked me to come to the Test Trial at Lord's. I played for England against The Rest—Struddy was the other keeper—and I kept as well as at anytime in my life against Tate, Gubby Allen, Macaulay, Kilner and Woolley. Arthur Gilligan said to me, 'Is that the first time you've kept to Maurice, Tiger?' I said, 'Yes, why?' and his reply was 'Because you make it look so easy.' I was very pleased with my display and Warner told me I'd be in the Test team. It was announced the next day and Struddy was in.

I was terribly disappointed because my hopes had been raised so high. I received no word of explanation from anyone. There were some funny selections in 1926—Struddy was dropped after a bad match at Lord's and they brought in, of all people, George Brown to keep wicket. Now George was a fine bat and a good fast bowler but he wasn't up to much as a keeper. George then broke a finger and instead of bringing in the man who kept in the Test Trial the selectors brought back the man they'd dropped—Struddy. I didn't begrudge Struddy his moment of glory at The Oval—I had mine in Australia with Johnny Douglas—but I was bitterly upset.

I realized how much I missed my old pals. Charlesworth and Hargreave. They'd have given me a rocket and told me to stop moping around. But from that heartache I learned something that helped me as an umpire and coach—you need an arm round you when you're doing badly. You don't need attention when things are going well. I got no sympathy from my fellow pros at Edgbaston, probably because I was a bit gruff and they thought I'd snap back at them but it was the only time in my career I felt sorry for myself. My batting fell away badly and I got under 500 runs that season, compared with nearly 1500 the season before.

Things were never quite the same for me as a player after that and my differences with the Warwickshire committee didn't help either. The fun was going out of my cricket. . . .

8
TIGER SMITH—TROUBLEMAKER?

My last few playing years at Edgbaston weren't happy ones. All the old pros had gone, my old chum Jack Parsons was now an amateur so I didn't see much of him, the new captain Bobby Wyatt and I didn't really get on, and then there was the secretary.

Now I agree I'm a gruff old devil who barks a bit and, believe me, I've always been the same. So I'm sure I gave the wrong impression to quite a few committeemen over the years at Edgbaston. Some of them were perfect gentlemen, but with many others it was 'How do, Tiger' if I'd done well and 'I want you Smith' if I'd done badly. Too many of them believed the tittle-tattle about me and the worst culprit was the secretary, R. V. Ryder.

'R.V.R.' and myself were never agreeable. I always tried to keep out of his way because he was a proper autocrat. He was the big noise at Edgbaston and though I admit he worked hard and knew his cricket, he had a finger in every-thing. He'd often change the side for away matches once the captain had picked the eleven.

There was the time when Len Bates was chosen for an away match but when he got there he found that Reggie Santall had got his place. It was a cock-eyed way to run a cricket club and to his credit, Bobby Wyatt wouldn't stand for 'R.V.R.'s' interference. He told him he wouldn't be skippered from the pavilion and as a reward the committee told Bobby he was going to be replaced by G. D. Kemp-Welch for the new season—even though Bobby had captained England against Australia the previous summer!

Thankfully that blew over but it shows the committee's mentality at the time.

The committee treated Billy Quaife shabbily in the end. Now Billy was almost as big a thorn in 'R.V.R.'s' flesh as I was. He had a living outside the game with his sports shop so he could afford to speak his mind. In 1921 he tried to get on the committee because he said his fellow-professionals had been treated badly in the past. He didn't get on, not surprisingly. Throughout the 'twenties Billy was rowing with the coach, Sid Santall, our former player. Billy and Sid both had sons and they wanted them to do well with Warwickshire. They both had a bee in their bonnets about their sons, particularly Billy, who couldn't seem to realize that Bernard wasn't a top-class player. His fielding was even worse than mine, and he was a young man.

And there were lots of whispers flying round that Reggie Santall got too many chances because of Sid's influence—although I must admit Reggie became a fine player and a great hitter of the ball.

By 1928 Billy was gone and I felt even more alone. The youngsters were coming through and they wanted to push the old birds out of the nest. Eventually I was happy to let them.

In the 'twenties I used to have a glass of beer before going out to play in the morning. It helped me sweat freely, something I always maintain a cricketer should do because that doesn't sap his nervous energy. Well, word spread that I was a boozer. 'R.V.R.' certainly believed the whispers because one day he shook his head and said to me, 'I don't know how you do it, Smith.' He didn't think I had the common sense to keep myself fit for cricket. . . .

Then there was the row over the drink chit. In the 'twenties the pros were allowed ninepence worth of drink, no spirits, at lunchtime. I always had half a pint of beer and then I'd sign for it. Well, one day someone had a few more drinks and signed my name on his chit. I got hauled over the coals by 'R.V.R.' who was convinced I was knocking back the booze. One of the umpires, A. E. Street, saw it all happen, yet when I asked him to confirm my story he said, 'Don't bring me into it.'

I was once reported for being rude to one of the club's oldest members and the committee took a very poor view of it. I'd scored a hundred against Essex in 1930 and when I was out I had a quick wash down and walked round to the bar and bought a glass of Guinness. I was just paying for it when this member came up and said 'I'll buy that, Smith.' I said, 'You come when I've got a nought'—the point I was making was that you need encouragement when you're in trouble not back-slapping when you've done well. But I was hauled off to the office, told I'd insulted the member, and Ryder said 'You're a funny fellow, Smith.'

'R.V.R.' also thought I was leading some of the young pros astray when we went on away games. What he didn't know was that I hardly ever stayed with them in their hotels. I always had a good bed and good breakfast when I played away, whereas some of the young pros liked to stay in Temperance hotels and bring crates of beer in at the dead of night. They didn't look too healthy in the mornings and 'R.V.R.' thought it was my fault.

I was blamed when a player was reported for being unfit for play at Tunbridge Wells in 1929. Jack Parsons the skipper that day was furious. I'd stayed in a separate hotel and when the committee quizzed me I pointed out I wasn't senior pro and, therefore, not their keeper. I said if I'd been in charge of them there'd be some discipline because in all my career I'd never once been unfit for cricket. J. F. Byrne, the former skipper, turned to 'R.V.R.' and said, 'You'll never get anything out of him until you give him authority.'

The unruly behaviour of some of the young players caused the big break the following year. We were playing Glamorgan at Swansea and for once all the pros were staying at the same hotel in Mumbles. I went out for a drink with a friend and when I got back there was a hell of a schemozzle. The hotel manager was trying to turf all the players out because three or four had been misbehaving. I quietened him down but he wrote to 'R.V.R.' and because I was then senior pro, I got the blame. None of the young pros would speak up for me so I had to take the rap.

That incident didn't make me want to play much longer and I played my final match at Leyton against Essex. Nobody knew it yet, but I was aware I was pulling on my flannels for the last time. I didn't feel at all nostalgic or sad, I just wanted 'out'. I had a nice house in Torquay, a small boat, two daughters at grammar school down there and my coaching in South Africa so I wasn't short. I may've been daft in other ways but I've been sensible with money . . .

In my last match I got a first innings fifty and then in my final knock I was caught for 7 by the young wicketkeeper Sheffield off Kenneth Farnes. I wasn't out actually—I didn't touch the ball, it clicked the off bail and when Frank Chester heard the click he thought it'd come from the bat. But I had no complaints; I was morally out because the ball had hit the wicket.

So that was it. The committee asked me to go and see them after the match but I went home to Torquay instead. They wrote and offered me a match contract of £12 per match. They knew I wouldn't accept that because I was 44, a liability in the field if I didn't keep wicket, and I probably wouldn't play more than three or four matches because Jack Smart was waiting to take over the gloves.

I wrote back, saying I didn't like the atmosphere, the way the side was being captained and that Jack Smart was ready to take over from me. So my career was over.

I had no regrets. Perhaps I should've bitten on my tongue a few times but I've always believed in being straight and honest. The pros were still being treated as serfs at Edgbaston in 1930 just as they had been when I started, and I didn't like that. The amateurs' expenses were far higher than ours and we found that out in an unusual way towards the end of my career. We were playing at Old Trafford and on the final day our expenses were sent up. As luck would have it, we got the amateurs' instead—well over £100 to be divided up among three of them. Freddie Calthorpe came in looking flustered and said, 'Have you got our exes, Tiger?' and handed over our envelope—£100 for nine pros. Quite a difference. . . .

So I wasn't sad to leave Edgbaston as a player. And 'R.V.R.' must've realized he'd been hard on me because the following summer he heard I was on the ground. He sent for me and said 'Good morning, Tiger' (he'd never called me that before) and he ordered two beers. Over the first drink I'd had with him in 26 years he leaned towards me and said, 'Tiger, I blamed you for a lot in the past. I know now that it wasn't your fault.' Obviously the ructions and the indiscipline were still going on. Anyway he told me to come and see him whenever I was on the ground, so we parted on good terms.

One thing pleased me in my final season—I scored a thousand runs, including three centuries, so I was still worth my place in the side. So twenty-six years of laughs, frustration, achievements and disappointments were over. I didn't realize it then but an even more rewarding period in my life was about to begin. . . .

9

UMPIRING DAYS

I learned more in my first year as an umpire than in all the previous twenty-six years of playing the game, and yet I'd never really thought about umpiring when I finished playing. Warwickshire had put my name forward and in December 1930 I was told by Lord's I was on the list for the next season.

I received no training: there were no exams or courses. The powers that be assumed I knew the Laws and all I had to do was turn up in my white coat at the start of the 1931 season. I earned roughly £10 a match—about the same as the players—and it was nice to meet up with some of my old pals who were now umpiring and to keep in touch with the game. I'd turned down the chance of coaching at Malvern and Eton Colleges—imagine that, the rebel 'Tiger' Smith coaching at posh schools—and the next few years were very happy.

My first game was at Taunton between Somerset and Hampshire and I was in the hot seat straight away. In a tight finish Somerset needed about twenty to win with their last pair together. Well, my old mate Alec Kennedy bowled the last over to Jack Lee and every ball was accompanied by a loud appeal from the bowler. I turned them all down and afterwards Alec said, 'You were right but I only wanted one more wicket for five wickets and talent money.' Alec knew it was a good idea to pressurize a new umpire, but he didn't realize that would never work with me. The more they barked at me the happier I was. I'd just say, 'You'll want a cough lozenge in a minute.'

George Macaulay tried it on with me the first time I stood

in a Yorkshire match that season. It was at Leeds against
Essex and I no-balled him because he was over the line—
but he didn't let go of the ball and showed it to me. The next
one I no-balled him again so George went down the wicket
and started scratching it up with his studs and glaring at me.
'If you do that again, you won't bowl this end any more,' I
said, and I told his skipper Frank Greenwood the same. I
told George, 'If you do that again I'll call it a no-ball even if
it's just a few inches outside the off stump.' After that
George was as good as gold.

I can't have been too bad as an umpire because within a
year I was standing in a Test Trial and the next season saw my
first Test. It was a pleasant change to be treated with such
respect by officials and players; as a player with a bit of a
reputation I was Jack the Ripper, but as an umpire I was
Mary Pickford to many. All of a sudden I'd become an elder
statesman. One or two skippers would try it on but we'd be
friends for life as soon as they saw I wouldn't be taken for a
ride. I well remember my first brush with Walter Robins
when he was bowling for Middlesex:

ROBINS: 'Howzat?'
SMITH: 'Not out.'
ROBINS: 'Howzat now?'
SMITH: 'Not out now.'
ROBINS: 'Well I think it should be.'
SMITH: 'So do I, but the Laws don't.'

After that, we were great pals . . .

I still didn't mince my words, though. Once at Lords I
was umpiring with Fanny Walden and I didn't get my lunch
until it was time to go back on to the field. A lot of bigwigs
were being entertained and there weren't enough waitresses.
I told Plum Warner I wasn't going out till I'd had my lunch.
I was had up in the office that night and asked why play had
re-started five minutes late—yet the next day the two
umpires and scorers were given their own table and their
own waitress.

Many times I've been asked if I felt frustrated out in the middle because I wasn't playing any more. Not once did I think, 'I could've hammered that ball' or 'I'd have snapped that one up.' I didn't miss playing at all. I got as much fun out of watching the respective skills as when I was playing. Now that I was no longer behind the stumps I could appreciate the batsmen's footwork more and I could see what the bowler was trying to do because I'd stand a good yard back from the stumps and watch the ball through the air.

That fine fast bowler Billy Bestwick summed it up for me when he was asked if he liked umpiring. 'It's grand,' he said, 'but there were many I had given out when I was bowling that weren't out.' And Billy was a really good umpire—he admitted he was still learning after years of umpiring.

I got a great kick out of watching young lads develop when I umpired and I'd often slip in a quiet word to a youngster when nobody else was listening on the field. I remember telling Jack Robertson he wasn't getting his right foot parallel to his body when he played back, which was making him simply an on-side player. I was delighted that Jack became such a fine off-side player and I hope my words helped. I know I was supposed to be neutral but I don't think anyone would've minded—cricket's the kind of game where you can help youngsters as an umpire yet you can still be respected as a fair-minded person.

So I was still closely involved in the game I loved. I'd become respectable even though I hadn't changed a bit. And I was with many of my old friends from years back. Men like Dick Burrows, Tommy Oates, Jack King, Len Braund and George Beet were all umpiring when I joined the list in 1931 but three stand out in my memory: Frank Chester, Billy Reeves and Alec Skelding.

Frank Chester did more for the game than any umpire I've known. Having lost an arm in the First War he came early to umpiring. He had a keen mind and was scrupulously honest and fair and he wouldn't be overawed by some of the amateurs who made a weak umpire's life such a misery. Nobody would ever tell Frank Chester what to do and he set new standards for the profession. I treasured Frank's remark to me the first time we stood together. 'I hope you do well, Tiger,' he said, 'because you were always fair as a player.' He was a fine man and I admired him greatly.

I admired Billy Reeves for having the quickest wit of any cricketer I knew. His quips were legendary. In my first away match at Leyton in 1905, he put Johnny Douglas in his place. Billy had chased a ball on that very large ground, the batsmen had run three and Billy was taking a long time to get back to his place. 'You've been gone a long time, Billy,' said Douglas. 'Ay, there wasn't a cab on the rank,' said Billy—and in those days the pro just didn't speak to an amateur like that. Billy would get away with murder because he was so likeable. There was the time when he displeased Walter Robins for turning down so many appeals. At the end of the over he offered Robins his Middlesex sweater with the three seaxes on the front. 'You know what you can do with that,' said Robins. Quick as a flash, Billy said, 'What, swords and all?'

A young amateur was given out by Billy and he didn't like it. The next interval he asked Billy why he'd given him out. Instead of tea and sympathy he got the reply, 'You were making such a fool of yourself I thought I'd put you out of your misery.'

Another amateur was upset by Billy giving him out. As he walked past he asked, 'What am I out for?' Quick as a flash Billy said, 'The rest of the bleedin' afternoon.'

Billy's vocabulary and cheek were huge. There was never a dull moment with him and he hated having to keep quiet in Test matches. He upset Alf Gover once after no-balling him for dragging. 'What an umpire,' said Alf as he walked back to his mark. Billy bided his time until Alf was past him and just as he was about to let the next ball go, he said in a loud voice, 'What a bowler!'

Alec Skelding was almost as great a card as Billy, although

Alec had a hell of a temper when roused. A tough nut, was Alec—he once put the famous black boxer Larry Gaines on his back in a fight, and I remember one match at Sheffield when Alec, by making very positive gestures, put the wind up the crowd for the rest of the match.

One of the first umpires to wear white boots, Alec was a very well-educated man who wrote some fine poems about an umpire's lot. He was a great wit and had a great way of telling a tale. Funny how so many great characters played for Leicestershire—George Geary was another. He had me in stitches once when he and the other bowlers were being hammered and he was getting a bit fed up. His skipper said, 'Who shall we put on next, George?'—'The clock, sir', replied George.

A lot of players could get het up in my day, just as they do today. A fair amount of gamesmanship went on when I was umpiring and despite Frank Chester's shining example, some umpires still buckled under pressure. A lot of this was due to the marking system at the time: you were given three grades—good, bad or indifferent—and if a captain gave you the bad grade three times in a row, you were struck off the list with no right of appeal. That was unfair because I've known at least two occasions where the unlucky umpire made the correct decision but was given a black mark by the skipper who'd lost the game. It was wrong that the umpire's career should depend on the mood of a captain he'd possibly offended.

I was reported once—by Percy Fender of Surrey. It was against Middlesex and I gave E. T. Killick 'not out' after Fender caught the ball at slip off Bob Gregory. The bat hit the ground and made a clicking sound but Killick made no contact with the ball. Fender wasn't pleased with my de-cision—and when I no-balled him several times shortly afterwards he was even less pleased. Fender complained to me and mentioned the Killick decision as well. I said, 'Do you think I'm a cheat then?' and I got the impression he thought I was. When he asked why I was no-balling him, I said 'Because your feet are too big.' That did it—'I'm reporting you, Smith,' he said, and at the end of the match I didn't get my money. When I was called up before the MCC secretary, Mr. Findlay, to explain myself, he laughed when I told him what I'd said about Fender's feet and he said, 'Well, he's got the complete set now. He's reported all of you—including Frank Chester.' And we had a good laugh. Shortly after that Mr. Findlay decreed that the umpires should always be paid after the second day's play . . .

Surrey weren't a pleasant side to umpire in those days. Fender liked his own way and the air was blue from the amateurs when things weren't going right. Like the Australians of recent years they'd take the mickey out of the batsmen to upset them and I know Jack Hobbs was happy to be out of it eventually. I was always glad to get away from The Oval in the 'thirties. It was a complete contrast to the other games. The attitude towards me by the other skippers of the time was summed up by Maurice Turnbull of Glamorgan. Someone told me once that when Maurice heard I was umpiring a Glamorgan match he said, 'Oh, you're all right, you can play with your legs today. If Tiger says you're out, then you're out.' I was very touched by that; it was typically generous of Maurice.

Very few players made a point of questioning my decisions. The most blatant piece of dissent came from my old Warwickshire colleague, Bobby Wyatt. It was in a Gents v Players match in 1939. I gave him out caught at the wicket off Bill Bowes, and halfway back to the pavilion, Bobby turned round and glared at me. Yet George Heane, the Notts skipper, who was batting at my end, said he was definitely out—and I believe George and Wally Hammond gave him a going-over in the dressing-room afterwards. Anyway in the second innings Bobby had to retire hurt after being battered about by Copson and Bowes—they didn't approve of his gesture either.

Of course I made mistakes, but I couldn't afford to brood about them. I'd take the decision on the basis of what I'd seen and heard and wouldn't be influenced by anybody. I remember Jim Parks trying to influence me in the 1937 season. Jim needed just a few more runs for his 3000 runs (he also took 100 wickets) and I signalled a leg-bye for a boundary. 'I played that, you know,' he said—'Well play it a bit harder next time, I didn't hear it,' I said.

I only once pondered about a decision I gave. I was at Lord's, Middlesex were playing Yorkshire, and I gave Hedley Verity out lbw. Hedley took the decision like the grand fellow that he was but he told me afterwards he thought the ball was going over the top of the stumps. I've often wondered since if Hedley was right.

I remember making an elementary error in my first season. It was the kind of mistake many an ex-player must make when he starts umpiring. It was at Worcester and the Leicestershire bowler Snary had an amateur batsman stumped by Tommy Sidwell. Trouble was I didn't see it from square leg because I was watching where the ball should've gone through the covers. The first I knew about the stumping was a lusty appeal from Bradshaw beside me—that's why I've been deaf in my right ear since. I said 'not out' and admitted afterwards to the skippers, Eddie Dawson and Cyril Walters, that I was at fault and they both had a good laugh about it. But it taught me a lesson—watch where the ball is, not should be.

One of the biggest strains on the umpires in the 'thirties was bodyline bowling—especially by the great Notts pair, Larwood and Voce. Well I can only speak as I found it, and in the games when I umpired them, I saw little that was unfair. Only once did I pull Bill Voce up—he was peppering the Gloucestershire last man, Williams, on his legs. Williams wasn't up to playing him and he was nearly treading on the square-leg umpire's corns. I said, 'It's about time you knocked the wickets over'—and straight away he did.

There was a lot of hysteria at the time about bodyline. I remember Lancashire sending a photo to Lord's of George Duckworth's left thigh looking like a piece of liver after facing Larwood and Voce. I had to point out that they'd been bowling at the stumps, not at George, who was a small man and whose stance was a bent-kneed, low one. All the hysteria had ignored the fact that the bowling hadn't been short-pitched, that George had a bat in his hand to hit the ball, and that if I'd thought the batsman was being intimidated I'd have had a word with the skipper.

Talking about bodyline brings me on to the first Test I umpired and the bravest innings I've ever seen. It was a hundred by Douglas Jardine at Old Trafford against the West Indian pace attack of Constantine, Martindale and Griffith. Jardine had returned from Australia a few months earlier, having won the Ashes by bodyline tactics, and the West Indians decided to give him a taste of his own medicine. I stood at the Stretford End and Martindale and Constantine, both bowling round the wicket, hit him time and again on the thigh and chest. Not once did Jardine complain. He never even rubbed where he was hit, although he dropped his bat a number of times. He wasn't wearing any padding yet four balls an over were short. I didn't like Jardine as a man—he was a throwback to the days of the autocratic amateur—but that day I was full of admiration for him.

It was certainly an interesting introduction to Test cricket for me. The other features in a rain-affected drawn match were a hundred for Ivan Barrow in his first Test and a century by George Headley. But it was Headley's high spirits at the end of the game I remember particularly clearly—he was so delighted that the mighty England had been held to a draw that he had a few celebratory beers and in very quick time, young George was distinctly the worse for wear.

Lord knows why I was selected for a Test within just two years of taking up umpiring. I certainly didn't buy anyone drinks. I was told a fortnight in advance and I was given £15, which was better than a smacked bottom . . .

The next Test I umpired was an historic one: South Africa's first win in England. It was at Lord's in 1935 and the highlight was a great attacking 90 by Jock Cameron. A few months later he died of typhoid, a great loss to us all. The joy of the South Africans was a delight to see at the end of the game, but England didn't play the turning ball at all well. A great character by the marvellous name of Xenephon Balaskas took nine wickets in the match with leg-breaks and googlies, quite a contrast to the performance of Tommy Mitchell for England. Tommy fell out with his skipper, Bobby Wyatt, who'd moved from the gully to mid-on to coach Tommy after he'd bowled Siedle out in his first over. Tommy got so fed up with Wyatt telling him what to send down that he told him to go on himself—with a few colourful adjectives thrown in—and he was taken off.

Hay-fever caused a late withdrawal from the England side just before the start. The unlucky player was the Oxford bat, N. S. Mitchell-Innes, and that grand fellow Errol Holmes of Surrey took his place. No offence to either man but it makes you think when there were such fine pros around like Eddie Paynter, Maurice Leyland and Wally Keeton who couldn't get a game.

My next Test was two years later at Old Trafford against New Zealand—and here I crossed swords again with the journalist E. H. D. Sewell. I hadn't thought much of him ever since he wrote Warwickshire off in the first match of our Championship season in 1911, and this time he criticized Billy Reeves and myself for moving the covers well away from the wicket to let the wind dry it out. When we saw that Sewell had criticized our knowledge of the Laws, Billy and I went straight to the Lancashire chairman, Tommy Higson, and complained. Sewell said he didn't think his paper would print an apology so Tommy Higson took his pavilion pass from him and told him to stay in the Press-box from then on.

The rain was the dominant feature of that match, although I remember the 21-year-old Len Hutton getting his first Test hundred. Only 15,000 turned up during the three days, but it was so cold and damp I wasn't surprised. I remember Jack

Cowie getting ten wickets in the match for the New Zealanders—he was a fine medium-pace bowler in the classic old style. Another fine bowler, Tom Goddard, took 6 for 29 to win the match for England. Tom had very long fingers. He bowled round the wicket and with his great height could really make the off-spinner bounce. But he never managed to conceal his quicker ball—he couldn't stop his stride getting wider when he bowled it.

I stood in the next Test at The Oval. It was Denis Compton's debut and I gave him out in controversial circumstances. He'd made 65 in his usual free and easy style when the ball was played back to the bowler, H. G. Vivian. Denis was at our end. Vivian deflected the ball on to the wicket, saw that Denis was only standing on the popping crease, not *inside* the crease, and appealed for a run-out. I gave Denis out straight away and Vivian then said he didn't mean to appeal. But once an appeal had been made and a decision given, there could be no change of mind and Denis grinned and accepted it.

Joe Hardstaff got a hundred in that match. Whenever Joe got runs they were always beautifully made. I never saw a better stance at the wicket than Joe's; the hands at the top of the handle and his upright stance meant that he could play the cut or drive easily and gracefully. His stance was a great contrast to Martin Donnelly's. Martin was pigeon-toed and he looked very curious before playing a ball—yet he got fifty in this Test and scored hundreds of graceful runs. He was proof that unorthodoxy didn't stop anyone being a classical bat.

The 1938 Australians were a different kettle of fish to the gentle inexperienced New Zealanders. I stood in two Tests that year—at Lord's and Headingley—and they were a hard bunch. Don Bradman was a strict disciplinarian and he kept his side in good order off the field, a pleasant change from some recent Australian sides, but the 1938 team overdid the gamesmanship. They'd appeal for lbws from cover point, none of them 'walked' when batting, and bowlers like

O'Reilly (I can't think why he was nicknamed 'Tiger') appealed so often I'd offer them cough lozenges. They were a clannish lot on the field. They'd never speak unless spoken to and yet they'd natter away at the umpires once play began. An umpire had to stand up to them and I'm sure you realize I was happy doing just that . . .

That Lord's Test sticks firmly in my mind; there was a superb double-hundred by Wally Hammond without giving a chance and a marvellous reception from the crowd. He shared a big partnership with Eddie Paynter that I really enjoyed because of their contrasting styles. I gave poor Eddie out lbw for 99; he went to pull a long-hop that didn't pitch halfway and he missed it completely. Eddie was furious with himself because he got excited; he could have played it easily away for a single.

Then there was Bill Brown carrying his bat through the Australians' first innings for a double-century. It wasn't a great innings though. Brown was a limited player with little to show on the offside. As a batsman he wasn't in the same street as Hammond or Bradman, never mind the same parish.

Bradman got a hundred in this match and it was the only time I saw him change colour. I was at square leg and Kenneth Farnes was really slipping himself from the pavilion end, where the light was never very good. Farnes bowled Bradman a fast, short one and he flinched out of the way just at the last instant. His face was turned towards me and it went as white as chalk . . .

Farnes had a go at me twice in the match when I turned down lbw appeals against Bill Brown. They both would've missed the leg stump by at least six inches. I told Kenneth to come and have a look from my vantage point. Then he grinned and said, 'You're right'.

I felt sorry for Ernie McCormick. I had to no-ball him time and again and after a couple of overs Bradman took him off. Poor Ernie was very annoyed with himself and never complained to me about being no-balled. Which is more than I can say for Bill O'Reilly (I shan't call him 'Tiger'). I called him when he followed through in Fleetwood-Smith's deep footmarks. 'They give me those in Australia,' said O'Reilly. 'Well you're not getting them here,' said the other 'Tiger'.

I couldn't quite work out why Plum Warner thought so highly of O'Reilly. At the end of that tour, Plum said he was another S. F. Barnes. I couldn't accept that. O'Reilly flighted the ball well but his deliveries were slower than his bounding run-up promised. He held the ball in his hands rather than his fingers, which meant he didn't spin it too much and the ball would go through the air slowly. Fingleton and Brown got him a few catches at short leg but I honestly don't think he was in the same class as Clarrie Grimmett.

The Leeds Test was a fine game of cricket. Australia needed only just over a hundred to win and lost five wickets, with Doug Wright giving them a fright. Bradman got a very good hundred, then got out to a wild stroke against Bill Bowes—and in the second innings he was caught at slip and stood there till Frank Chester said, 'You've been out a fortnight.' O'Reilly got ten wickets in the match, including Wally Hammond first ball when he played a firm-wristed, tame shot to short leg. Eddie Paynter and Bill Edrich played deliveries on to their wickets, yet didn't dislodge the bails—Bradman couldn't believe it. The wicket was described as 'sporting' by the critics and the knowledgeable Yorkshire crowd loved the tense battle.

Two Tests involving West Indies in 1939 brought my total up to eight and I enjoyed them all. There was more fun and wisecracks in the county games—often I never had a chat with any overseas fielder during a Test—but it was fascinating to see the great international players at close quarters. I didn't find it more mentally tiring than in the county games because I always took a decision on its merits and didn't worry about repercussions.

Apart from the Tests, I stood in some famous matches in the 'thirties. There was the Essex/Yorkshire match at Leyton in 1932 when Holmes and Sutcliffe set the new record of

555 for the first wicket. And yet if I hadn't remembered a no-ball the record wouldn't have been established. All hell broke loose after Herbert Sutcliffe dragged a wide one from Laurie Eastman on to his stumps as soon as the openers had set the new record. Herbert had clearly thrown his wicket away because the ball was nearly a wide and he played it casually. While he and Percy Holmes were posing for photographs beside the scoreboard it was discovered that the scorers hadn't done their sums properly and they'd only made 554. Well Frank Field and myself were asked if we remembered anything and I said, 'Did you get the no-ball?'

The first delivery of the second day from Arthur Daer I called a no-ball and although the scoreboard had put it up, the Essex scorer (Charlie McGahey) had missed it. Arthur Daer confirmed it—and the record was saved. The only reason why I remembered that no-ball was because the same thing had happened on the first day—the same bowler (Daer), the same batsman (Holmes), the same stroke (a push to mid-on), and the same umpire (myself).

Down the years people have said 'Oh Tiger, surely you felt sorry for the batsmen and you fiddled it?' That's not true; if they'd given me a thousand quid I wouldn't have fiddled it. I did get something out of that match though. At the time there was a popular cigarette on the market called State Express 555. Well, the manufacturers knew a good piece of free advertising when they saw it and they sent the players, scorers and umpires loads of free fags to commemorate the great occasion. They were a good smoke too. . . .

Another match involving Yorkshire was the worst one I ever umpired. It was against Middlesex and with both sides neck-and-neck for the Championship the ingredients for a hell of a battle were already there. Then on the first morning on a typically dodgy Lord's wicket, Laurie Gray and Jim Smith put three men out of action—Paul Gibb (fractured skull), Len Hutton (broken finger) and Maurice Leyland (broken thumb). And when Walter Robins told Brian Sellers that if Leyland batted with his arm in a sling 'He'll get no sympathy from me' that really did it.

When 'Robbo' came in to bat, Bill Bowes asked to bowl and he really went for his man. The ball kept following Robbo's body and he ended up playing from square leg. (I've had corns ever since.) I don't know what got into 'Robbo' that day—he and Sellers fell out before the start because when Yorkshire won the toss, 'Robbo' pointed out they hadn't tossed up standing on the grass but in the pavilion and could they do it again. Sellers told him where to go and that set the tone. Eventually Middlesex got what they wanted—a handsome victory against eight men—but if ever an old-timer tries to tell you there was no intimidation or bad blood in his day, just mention Middlesex/Yorkshire 1938. . . .

But my memories of umpiring are happy ones. We had many laughs—not least the dodges some umpires used to get off the field when the lunchtime beer had caught up on us and we needed to spend a penny. Frank Chester had an ingenious ploy. He'd always carry a broken bail so that he could substitute that and then say he had to nip in and change it. Trouble was that if Frank scarpered the other umpire couldn't go as well, so I used to bring a little bottle out with me and when nobody was looking I'd fill that up. Failing that I'd take a walk round at square leg and hope nobody saw what was trickling on to the grass. I always wore dark trousers just in case. We didn't let on to the players because somebody might've stopped us having a beer at lunch . . .

The controversial 'snick' rule in the mid-thirties caused a few laughs on the county circuit, chiefly because of one umpire, George Brown, the former Hampshire all-rounder. The 'snick' rule said that the batsman was out lbw even if he'd snicked the ball provided the ball would, in the umpire's opinion, have gone on to hit the wicket. It was a bad rule and caused a lot of trouble but it gave George Brown a golden opportunity to pay back a few old debts. He gave almost everyone out whenever there was an lbw appeal—especially against bowlers who'd 'done' him when he was a player! It became ridiculous. The batsmen were scared to get their pads near the stumps when George was umpiring. Many of George's matches were over in two days. Several skippers complained and he was quickly booted off the list—but he'd had a lot of fun in a short time.

Emmott Robinson looked at his umpire's duties differently. He didn't believe in giving batsmen out lbw. He only stood in one Test and he told me afterwards, 'I didn't do badly, Tiger, I didn't give anyone out.' I bet a match with George and Emmott umpiring would've been interesting . . .

Yes we had some laughs and I'm sure today's umpires enjoy still being involved with the game. In my day, and I think it's still true, the best umpires were English because they got regular practice at a high standard, and many of them were former players who knew the tricks of their trade. It's an even harder job now because the Press and television are always on the umpire's back, but I'm sure today's umpires are as philosophical as we were about errors. You've got to be calm and sensible about mistakes, otherwise you'd be a nervous wreck. One thing I say to the county captains—before the proper season starts you should stand in a match just to see how much the umpire has to cope with. Perhaps then you won't be so quick to blame the defects of your side on the poor old chap in the white coat.

1. Three stalwarts of
Warwickshire County
Cricket Club: (*above
left*) Sydney Santall,
(*above*) Frank Field
and (*left*) the
Hon. F. S. G. Calthorpe.

2. E. J. Smith keeping wicket for Warwickshire.

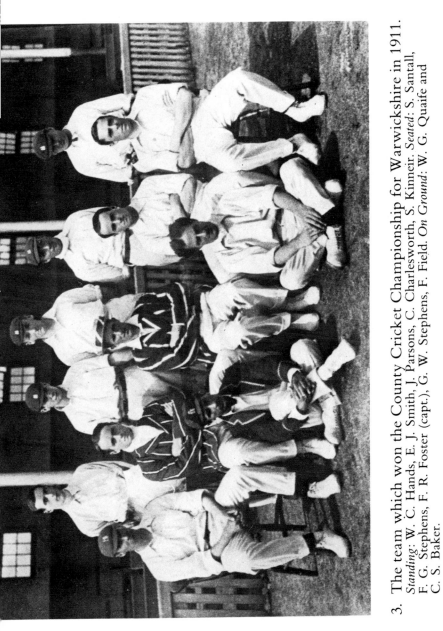

3. The team which won the County Cricket Championship for Warwickshire in 1911. *Standing*: W. C. Hands, E. J. Smith, J. Parsons, C. Charlesworth, S. Kinneir. *Seated*: S. Santall, F. G. Stephens, F. R. Foster (capt.), G. W. Stephens, F. Field. *On Ground*: W. G. Quaife and C. S. Baker.

4. Frank Foster during his captaincy in the 1911
Championship season.

1 S. P. Kinnear.   2 J. W. Hearne.   3 T. Pawley, manager.   4 J. Iremonger.
5 H. Strudwick.   6 F. E. Wooley.   7 P. F. Warner, captain.
8 J. W. H. T. Douglas.   9 G. Gunn.   10 E. J. Smith.   11 W. R. Rhodes.
12 S. F. Barnes.   13 C. P. Mead.   14 J. B. Hobbs.   15 F. R. Foster

The MCC Touring Team to Australia for the 1911–12 Test series.

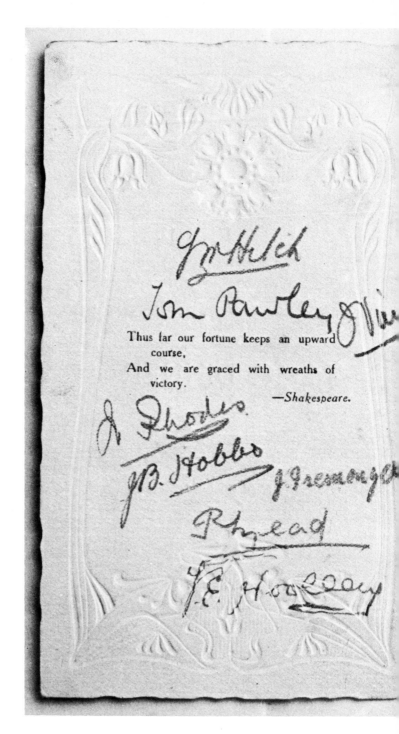

Thus far our fortune keeps an upward course,
And we are graced with wreaths of victory.

—*Shakespeare.*

6. The menu card for the Victory Dinner at the Hotel autographs.

MENU

"On a good wicket."

Hearne Bay Oyster Cocktails.
"First wicket down."

Turtle Soup au Douglas *(slow but sure)*
"How's that?"

Rhodes Schnapper a la Century
"Going great Gun(n)s."

Foster-ed Barn(es) Chicken au Maiden
"Clean bowled!"

Champagne Punch a la Campbell
"All out to Pommery '04."

Saddle Woolley Lamb and Vine Sauce
"Still no Hitch."

Hobb-led Asparagus and Pawley Dressing
"Another boundary."

Peche Warner
"Plums out of season."

Smith behind Marylebone Stumps
"Ashes on toast."

entworth, Sydney, February 27, 1912. Note the famous

7. (*left*) The 'butler' made famous by P. G. Wodehouse was named after Percy Jeeves, a Warwickshire cricketer of great potential who was killed in the First World War. (*below*) A *Birmingham Post* cartoon of 'Tiger' Smith before his benefit match against Lancashire.

THE LADY OF THE ROSE.

LANCASHIRE

[Smith, the Warwickshire wicket-keeper, will take his benefit to-morrow, when Lancashire will be the visitors; and yesterday a deputation from Lancashire waited on the Prime Minister to protest against the proposed duty on German fabric gloves.]

Smith: "Welcome Miss, we won't discuss cotton gloves to-day."

8. (*above*) Return of
   MCC from
   South Africa,
   Southampton,
   March 31, 1914,
   l to *r* Mr. &
   Mrs. J. H. Hearne
   and Mr. & Mrs.
   E. J. Smith.

(*left*) R. V. Ryder,
Secretary of
Warwickshire CCC,
1895–1944.

THE WARWICKSHIRE COUNTY CRICKET TEAM.
(1923).

9. 1923 picture of the Warwickshire first team.
Standing: A. J. Croom, J. Smart, E. J. Smith, F. R. Santall, L. A. Bates,
H. Howell. *Sitting*: W. G. Quaife, G. W. Stephens,
F. S. G. Calthorpe (capt.), R. E. S. Wyatt, N. E. Partridge.

1924. Six famous names in Warwickshire cricket . . .
'Tiger' Smith, Willie Quaife, Freddie Calthorpe, Jack Parsons,
Len Bates and Harry Howell.

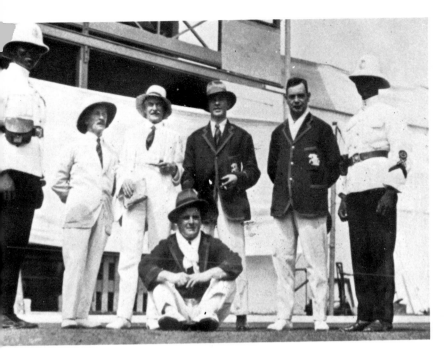

Two photographs of 'Tiger' at Barbados during his 1925–26 tour. In the top picture 'Tiger' is hatless.

11. The famous incident when umpire Smith gave Paynter lbw to O'Reilly when the batsman had scored 99. England *v.* Australia Test, Lords, 1938.

Smith as coach, helped to re-build the Warwickshire side in 1946.
Standing: W. E. Hollies, W. E. Fantham, H. E. Dollery, E. J. Smith, M. Barker, K. A. Taylor, N. A. Shortland. *Sitting*: R. Mead-Briggs, C. S. Dempster, P. Cramner (capt.) C. C. Goodway, C. H. Adderley.

2. 'Tiger' Smith coaching in the newly opened Edgbaston Indoor School 1956.

The Warwickshire CCC 2nd Eleven of 1953
Standing: J. L. Franklin (scorer), Tom Cartwright, Brian Lobb, Keith Dollery, Ian King, Jim Stewart, Don Taylor, Derief Taylor, Ray Hitchcock, and E. J. Smith (coach).
Sitting: Jimmy Ord, Maurice Robinson, Cyril Goodway (capt.), J. B. Guy and Ray Weeks.

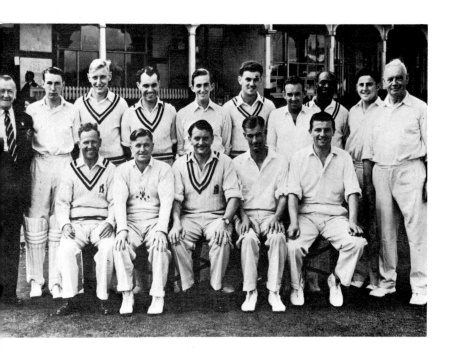

13. 'Tiger', the Warwickshire Coach, photographed in the changing rooms of the Edgbaston Indoor Cricket School at the opening on July 16, 1956.

4. (*above*) Alan Oakman, the present coach of Warwickshire,
with Canon Jack Parsons and 'Tiger', enjoying a day's
play at Edgbaston.
(*below*) Celebrations of the third winning by
Warwickshire of the County Cricket Championship. *l.* to
r. E. J. Smith representing the 1911 winners; Dennis Amiss,
the 1972 winners; and Tom Pritchard, the 1951 winners.

15. 'Tiger' talking cricket in the corner of the Players' dining
room. It is a picture to evoke happy memories of this man
whose bark was so decidedly worse than his bite.

10

COACH FOR WARWICKSHIRE

My appointment as coach for the 1946 season at Edgbaston came as a complete surprise; I'd spent many happy years coaching schoolboys in South Africa and I had a short spell at Worcester in 1935 but I'd no idea that the Warwickshire committee saw me as the man to help the captain Peter Cranmer put the side back on an even keel after the War. It was a great challenge and with Leslie Deakins always an agreeable and thoughtful secretary I had great satisfaction seeing my young lads develop. For ten years I was coach and then for another twelve I ran the indoor school with Derief Taylor, and I can't have been too bad at it because we won the Championship in 1951 and I had a hand in the development of players like Dennis Amiss, Tom Cartwright, David Brown, Jim Stewart, John Jameson and Bob Barber.

As a player I believed in attacking the ball and I didn't change my mind when coaching. I remember helping Bob Barber change his style after he came down from Lancashire. He was a stodgy, defensive player and I took him to the indoor nets and told him, 'You can no more play defensively than a schoolboy', made him play his shots and within a year he was in the England side and helping Warwickshire win the Gillette Cup.

It was the same with John Jameson; I simply encouraged him to hit the ball when he came to us from Taunton School. John's an intelligent man but I had to drum into him that he was a good player and it took some time for him to blossom, and he became as good an attacking opener as Charlie Barnett and Harold Gimblett. John still sends me a

Christmas card every year and so does Tom Cartwright, whom I coached when he was still at school. Tom was a natural bowler; when I first saw him swinging it both ways in the nets I told him just to work at his accuracy and to develop stamina. He had all the qualities but he lacked confidence and wasn't over-strong. So my job was to be gentle with him, to persuade the committee he was a fine bowler as well as a good batsman and keep hoping Tom's enthusiasm remained high. I'm delighted to say it did and his success gave me great pleasure.

I suppose it must sound strange that gruff old Tiger was gentle with some of the boys. Well it's true I was a strict disciplinarian and I expected high standards of dress and behaviour but I realized there was no point in bawling out a shy, sensitive youngster in front of the other boys. I'd put my arm round the lad and say in as kind a way as I could, 'If ever you want to ask me something, don't be afraid.' Now I'm sure many were afraid to ask but I always tried to be fair and I'd stand up for them if anyone else dared criticize them. I remember when Jim Stewart and Jack Bannister were just boys, playing for the Club and Ground. They were reported for some horse-play but after talking to them I was sure they hadn't behaved badly and I made sure their careers weren't harmed. I vividly recall one occasion when I stuck up for my boys—I was umpiring in a Club and Ground match at Belper and Denis Smith, the former Derbyshire batsman, kept giving our lads out every time there was an appeal. I got furious because these games were important for a youngster's development, so I ended up 'doing a Denis Smith' and by the end of the match I was ahead 7:6 on terrible decisions.

One of the qualities I looked for in a young player was intelligence, the ability to listen, to sift relevant information, apply it to one's own game and come back with questions if the advice wasn't understood. Cricket's a natural game but it also needs mental strength, something I had to learn the hard way because I had very little education and had to pick things up as I went along. The ability to take a telling-off in the right spirit is also a sign of intelligence and I certainly put the youngsters through some severe tests over the years. Mind you, I can't understand how they'd be frightened of a little old man like me. . . .

A coach must always be fair, he must never be seen to have favourites, even though he tries to treat certain boys differently from others. I always tried to mix with my players and hope they'd be fair to me. I was lucky in those days because the young lads weren't as forward as they are now. Many were straight from school or the Forces and my disciplinarian ways weren't all that strange. I'd crack down when I thought it necessary—once Jim Stewart and Fred Gardner came late to the nets. They were due on the ground at 11 from Coventry but they missed the train. I told them I wanted them to bowl at a member from 6 till 7 at night so it was fairly late before they got home. They didn't come late again and I think such discipline made them better players.

We were a happy family in those post-war years. Some of the team would pull my leg but they knew I'd be strict when necessary and the way they've all kept in touch proves I wasn't that much of an ogre. Only once did I have to report a player to the committee; it was Don Taylor, that fine New Zealand batsman. Don was a little older than the rest and he took me on at Preston when playing for the seconds. Our scorer had tickets for the Blackpool Tower that night and Don said he wanted to go along. I said he couldn't because he'd be out late and not fit for cricket the next day. Well, Don deliberately threw his wicket away when he was 96, told me he was going to Blackpool, and woke me up at three in the morning with a serenade outside my door. I smiled, said nothing to him and then a few days later in the nets at Edgbaston came another confrontation. I was watching him with a committee member, who said, 'I wish you could do something with him.' I asked a lad to bowl one at Don and told him to play it to mid-on. He swore at me, the committee member was shocked, and shortly afterwards

91

Don left the staff. Before leaving Don said he wished he'd taken more notice of me but you can't make disciplinary exceptions, no matter how good the player, because team spirit would be ruined.

Any credit for my success as a coach must be shared with that valuable servant, Derief Taylor. Although Derief didn't make the grade as a player just after the War, he's done so much for the youngsters at Warwickshire. He's a born teacher; where my manner frightened some of the boys, Derief had this quality of making them think he was only interested in their success. He was absolutely invaluable to me especially for the way he'd bowl a good line and length in the nets. If I was trying to make a boy improve his off-driving or master the square cut, I'd ask Derief to drop the ball on the required length and he could bowl that same delivery all day if necessary. I always insisted that the nets were the place to work, not to lark around and hit the cover off the ball—and Derief was marvellous at demonstrating the practical aspects.

Derief helped me spot the main weakness of Dennis Amiss when he first came to the nets as a boy. He couldn't play fast bowling and would back away to square leg far too often. He couldn't adjust to the change from the slow ball to the faster one, then to the really quick one. So we pushed a stick in the ground just behind his heels and got the fast bowlers to pitch them on his middle and leg. Whenever Dennis stepped over the stick he knew he wasn't facing up properly and he'd catch an earful from us. So he became a very fine player off his legs and one day, when he'd scored a hundred for Birmingham Boys at Edgbaston and Leslie Deakins said 'You want to get hold of that boy', I was proud to inform Leslie he'd been in the nets with us all that previous winter. Dennis had other assets that set him apart— he was strong-willed at an early age and although I've had cause to tell him off a few times for being selfish, his success has been due in no small degree to his determination and ability to keep his eyes and ears open.

Derief also helped me in the development of that great-hearted fast bowler, David Brown. He was always a strong lad and Derief supervised his training to give him the strong stomach and neck muscles and supple back that all fast bowlers need. But we had to fight to stop David being rushed too quickly into the county game; we held him back for two years even though the county needed a young fast bowler. If they'd put David in too early his physique couldn't have stood the daily pounding and Warwickshire would never have had a thousand wickets from a man who's been a great credit to the game, on and off the field.

After being in the game so long you tend to rely on certain guidelines in your assessment of a player's potential and for me one of the most important is the ability to field well. I've always appreciated good fielding, not least because all those years behind the stumps meant I could never be swift enough about the field, and I've often backed a hunch about a youngster because he was keen and quick as a fielder. Norman Horner, that graceful Yorkshire opener, was a case in point: I umpired in his first trial for us and he fielded beautifully. But when he came to bat, he made nought. He was walking away looking crestfallen when I shouted to him, 'Get back in there, we've come to see if you can play cricket.' He made a fine fifty and my hunch had paid off. Then Derief and I set out to cure his weakness against fast bowling. We'd get the fast men to bowl at him from 15 yards to sharpen up his reflexes and stop him backing away from the short-pitched stuff. He improved enormously, and became a very attractive opener who'd think nothing of cutting the first ball of the match for a boundary.

In case you think my time as coach and in the indoor nets was one long success story, I must point out we made many mistakes. Although we developed a nursery school for young talent it wasn't firmly established in time for the lean years that inevitably happen after a Championship win—in our case, 1951. Too many of the first team got complacent after we won the title and as Derief and I didn't have a say in selection, we couldn't get enough young lads in the side to keep the older ones on their toes. And we missed out on several bowlers who took thousands of first-class wickets between them—men like Vic Canning, Brian Crump, Jack Flavell, 'Butch' White and Ken Higgs. All of them were either on our staff or about to sign, but for a variety of reasons Warwickshire never got much out of them.

The Ken Higgs case was a sad one—I coached him for two years and after he came out of the Forces I went to see him play for Staffordshire against Cheshire. I thought highly of him because his second spell just before tea was as fast as his first one and at tea I phoned Edgbaston asking for permission to engage him. But we didn't do a thing for eight weeks and eventually he joined Lancashire and they and Leicestershire benefited from the skills I knew would make him an England bowler. We missed out on Colin Milburn as a youngster although at the time I wasn't too bothered because he was overweight and too vulnerable to the well-pitched-up delivery on his leg and middle sticks.

But such frustrations were outweighed by the thrill of seeing a boy make the grade after being under my wing. Some of the happiest days of my life have been spent learning to understand youngsters and trying to get them to understand me in the nets. I've been more elated at seeing men like Dick Spooner, Tom Cartwright, Dennis Amiss, Bob Barber, David Brown and John Jameson play for England than anything I've done in my playing or umpiring career. I felt I was passing on the knowledge I'd been lucky enough to glean from men like Quaife, Douglas, Hobbs, Rhodes and Hammond, and it was a great thrill to repay some of that debt. I'm sure I gave the wrong impression to some of the players when I was coach because I've always been a gruff old devil but I loved working with them and I was a sad man when I had to finish at the indoor school—after all I was only 82. . . .

Now that I've given up hope of ever becoming a great

off-spinner I sit and watch the cricket at Edgbaston and on the television with my beloved Rose—and many's the time I give her an ear-bashing about the daft tactics or the poor techniques of the batsman. That's one of the great advantages of being old, you don't have to stand up and put your theories to the test against Barry Richards, Thomson or Lillee. But I still find myself instinctively taking the ball when it passes the bat and I still wish I could have a few minutes in the nets with that youngster with the crooked pick-up, and why can't that lad stand up straight when he's delivering the ball, and why's the keeper standing back a pitch length for a medium-pacer, and what's the point in having six men on the off when he keeps spraying it outside the leg peg. . . .

11
WORLD XI

Every cricket fan plays this game at some stage, so for the first time in my life, I'll pick my all-time World team. And a difficult job it is, I can tell you. When you've been involved in the game since 1896 you've seen a fair old number of great players and it's been a privilege to do so. I've sat and thought about scores of men from all over the world I've admired and I've had to be ruthless in my selections. I must point out that my eleven players aren't necessarily the greatest cricketers I've seen. They've all been judged at the height of their powers, of course, but a good cricket team needs balance—balance in the batting order, in the field and in the bowling department—so this side is picked to win a game as a team, not just as a collection of talented individuals.

Nine of my side are more or less automatic choices. The difficulty comes with the last two places and keeping the balance just right. But the first name in the batting order is the obvious one—Jack Hobbs. He was the greatest all-round batsman I've seen, season in season out, on all types of wickets, anywhere in the world. He was so cool, masterful and relaxed, even though I've seen him totter at the crease many times because he was suffering from migraine. Once Jack got off the mark he was never worried—he'd turn to me behind the stumps and say 'I shan't bag 'em now' and he'd then proceed to play naturally. Today Test batsmen are often in for over four hours to make 70 and at the end their timing's little better than at the start.

Jack was a genuinely unselfish batsman; he'd never steal the bowling at the end of the over unless the other batsman

96

needed protection and many times I've seen him give his wicket away to the bowler he thought deserved it. He had no weakness and if he wanted to stay in, you'd need God on your side to get him out. He was an excellent judge of a run and many times he'd pick off four an over on a bad wicket when the bowler thought he was keeping him quiet. Jack's style changed after the Great War—before, he was as brilliant as Victor Trumper, with plenty of lofted drives and dazzling footwork. Afterwards he played the ball more on the ground and developed his masterful style. I think Jack was at his best in the 1920s—with men like Astill, Geary, Tate, Mailey, McDonald, Larwood, Kennedy and Newman and others around, the bowling was more varied and demanding than before the War.

As a fielder, Jack was one of the best cover points I've seen. Safe, swift and accurate, he was as ideal a model for youngsters in the field as with the bat. Modest, quiet and thoroughly decent, he was deservedly popular and did much to raise the reputation of the professional cricketer.

So who partners Hobbs? There are three candidates—Sutcliffe, Hutton and Woodfull. I go for Sutcliffe because he knew Jack very well, he faced better bowling in England during the 'twenties than the other two, and he was an excellent runner between the wickets. Woodfull was very solid, with the ideal opener's temperament, and Len was a fine bad-wicket player with a more elegant stance than Herbert—but Sutcliffe was so unflappable. He'd drive the bowlers mad because of this priceless ability to forget about the ball that nearly bowled him and concentrate on hammering the next one for a boundary. But Herbert's association with Hobbs is crucial.

First wicket down? No question about it—Bradman. On good wickets he was the most consistent of all. He wasn't a stylist, more a merciless player who punished anything loose and, because of his wonderful eye and reflexes, much that was respectable. He was a selfish batsman, but he could score his runs very quickly and that's always a priceless asset for a side because it means you get the opposition batting sooner. He didn't loft the ball unless he knew what he was doing—a very intelligent man, his quick brain helped him size up a situation so he could be relaxed when playing the shot. Bradman could move in any direction at the crease that split-second earlier than the others, so that he was in position to play the rising ball through cover or pull the good-length delivery. A bowler really had to bowl to his field when Bradman was around and I'd love to have seen a tussle with him and Syd Barnes in his prime. Syd would've thrown the ball up and invited Bradman to hit him and Don would've used his concentration and iron determination to make sure Barney didn't out-think him.

Many modern players don't believe Bradman would score so heavily today, with the more sophisticated field placings and the slow over rate. I believe this: if he came back today he'd have a picnic. He'd score many runs against bowlers who can't bowl at the stumps. People say he was weak on dodgy wickets but to be fair to him Bradman didn't see many of them. I think that he would've mastered bad wickets if he'd played over here regularly because his concentration, determination, reflexes, selection of strokes and co-ordination were so remarkable. I saw him play one great innings on a bad wicket—at Leeds in 1938, when his century held the side together against Bill Bowes and Doug Wright. After that day, I'd no doubts about Bradman's ability when the ball was playing tricks.

If he had a weakness, I think it was against top-class spin bowlers. He seemed happier against the quicker men because his eye and footwork were so good but I've seen Verity, Hollies and Jack White all troubled him. But Bradman was some player . . .

So was my number four batsman—Wally Hammond, second only to Jack Hobbs in my opinion. Twenty-two years after I started in first-class cricket, Wally made me look a cart-horse, and that day in West Indies made me realize just what's involved in being a great batsman. Wally was simply majestic. A lovely relaxed stance with so many different attacking shots available for any delivery, he looked as if he had a week of Sundays to play the ball. He was a great offside player and I never ceased to admire his ability to place the ball just wide of the fielder. His timing and power were tremendous and don't let anybody tell you he was weak on the leg side. The Aussies got him out once or twice on the leg side off Bill O'Reilly but Wally's footwork and placing meant he could pick off the boundaries all round the wicket.

I never saw him do an awkward thing on the field. A natural games player with a majestic walk, it was something just to see him walk on the field. And a great all-rounder—he was a fine bowler, as quick as Chris Old with a smooth, ten-yard run and genuine outswinger. As a slip fielder, he was marvellous and I've seen nobody better. His marvellous eye helped him see which way the ball was going and he got hundreds of wickets for Charlie Parker and Tom Goddard by anticipating a snick and moving to a certain spot before the ball had ever hit the edge of the bat. Wally Hammond was sheer class in everything he did. . . .

On to the all-rounders now and my vote goes to Gary Sobers. He'd flourish in any cricketing era I've known because he was a natural. Although a fine bowler he was best as a batsman, especially off his legs. Quite simply he put bat to ball and it was always a pleasure to watch Gary. He was lucky to be brought up on good fast wickets in the West Indies but like the old-timers he could score quickly against negative field placing and bowlers. Gary was always good for a three-hour Test hundred because he played the ball on its merits and gave it a good whack. I suppose most people think of his 36 runs in an over with all those sixes against Glamorgan—but I thought he was lucky that day because at least three of the sixes were just wild slogs. I prefer to remember him in Test matches, making it look an easy game while the other batsmen struggled.

Gary was a good spin bowler. He could spin the ball,

although he lacked accuracy, but he was better bowling fast. He had a lovely, flowing action and was really dangerous with the new ball. He had this knack of sending down a very late outswinger followed by a nasty in-ducker next ball—just ask Geoff Boycott about Sobers and the new ball. He was often compared to Alan Davidson but I thought Gary superior because he was more relaxed and lithe and as a result less prone to injury.

I'll leave the other all-rounder positions till later and my next automatic choice is Syd Barnes. I never saw a better bowler; he could bowl on all sorts of wickets, and deliver any type of ball. He was fascinating to keep wicket to but difficult to classify; Barney could bowl fast-medium, spin or cutters, all off the same run-up. Now and again he'd bowl the leg-break but his movement from the leg stick was primarily due to the cutter. A marvellously confident bowler, Barney wasn't a miser. He'd love to be hit for a boundary because that meant in his eyes that the batsman was getting over-confident and riding for a fall. What I admired so much about Barney was the way he'd attack a batsman as soon as he came in. If that didn't work, he'd alter his field after looking at the batsman's grip and stance and then hammer away at any weaknesses. And woe betide any fielder who strayed away from his position. Barney would have a few words to say if the ball went where he expected it to go and his man wasn't at home. Because of the force of his personality Barney could overwhelm many batsmen— how well I remember him doing just that in South Africa on the 1913–14 tour. I've never seen a bowler dominate sides so much. Many batsmen couldn't wait to get away down the other end, yet he was very unlucky to get only 49 wickets in four Tests because the matting wickets didn't help him.

The wicket-keeper in my side didn't need much thought— Bertie Oldfield. He was everything a keeper should be— quiet, alert, calm and near faultless. Dick Lilley was first rate; so was Les Ames, but Bertie was the best in my eyes.

His footwork was superb, his movements so smooth that he was never out of position. He stood up to the stumps far more than the modern keepers and the way he could take difficult bowlers like O'Reilly, Grimmett and Mailey proved his class. A useful bat as well, Bertie was a gentleman who was admired and loved by everyone.

Clarrie Grimmett gets in my side as the main spin bowler. He was so accurate and deadly on a wicket that gave him some help because he had the good sense not to spin it too much. On a bad wicket, he'd raise his arm a little higher, cut down on the spin, keep the ball well up and occasionally try for more bounce—and that was normally all that was needed. With his low trajectory he was normally just short of a length and very difficult to force away. His line was normally leg and middle but with his low action he could slide it across the right-hander with no change in delivery. Clarrie had a very good googlie and could bowl for long periods because he was so phlegmatic. Unlike O'Reilly he didn't fly off the handle; he was philosophical about dropped catches and didn't natter at the batsman to try to put him off. Clarrie was quicker than Benaud or O'Reilly but slower than Doug Wright and was a real thinker about the game. And with Bertie Oldfield behind the stumps in my side, Clarrie would be a happy man . . .

My main fast bowler's no trouble to me—Harold Larwood. He was the quickest I've seen, and remember he was up against some great batsmen in his time on wickets that were usually very flat and easy-paced. Unlike many English fast bowlers, he got wickets in Australia and such was his accuracy that a large percentage of them were clean bowled. Harold was as strong as a horse—he'd bowl eight overs at the start, come back after lunch and then at the end of the day be just as quick. From a twenty-yard run he'd come straight in and take a very long final stride. His great speed came from a fine body action. Like many fast bowlers he often didn't know where the ball would end up or whether it would swerve, but often the ball didn't have time to swing because it would rocket off the wicket.

101

A lot's been made over the years about Harold being an intimidating bowler; that wasn't true. He was as good as gold to play against. He'd almost always keep the ball well up to the bat and Harold would certainly have no time for today's intimidation.

Harold didn't have the best fast bowler's run-up I've seen; that was Ted McDonald's. He'd just glide in easily and elegantly and he was a glorious sight. But I pick Harold because he was more capable of getting rid of the first three batsmen while, on occasions, Ted would bowl too short when he lost his temper and could be picked off by the class batsman.

Two places to go then and time to take stock. I've got Larwood opening the bowling with Barnes or Sobers and to back them up there's Grimmett, Hammond and Sobers again with spin. I need another batsman and a class all-rounder. Two men contest the batting place—Denis Compton and Clive Lloyd. Both had that explosive quality the crowds love but I'm going to give it to Lloyd because of his superior fielding. Denis, of course, was a great player, a wonderful improviser. I remember umpiring a Middlesex match in 1938 when he scored 180 not out. It was one of the most audacious innings I've ever seen. I can still see his footwork. He was just never at home; he'd walk down the wicket and play the fast men through the covers just like George Gunn playing Cotter or McDonald. If Denis was around today, he'd be in clover, believe me. But Lloyd plays straighter; he's a model for youngsters to copy. Many's the time I've sat watching him on television and said to my wife, Rose, 'I hope the boys are watching this.' He's given me more pleasure than any other batsman in recent years because he's such a naturally correct hitter. His long reach helps him get to the pitch of the ball and his body and arms are in perfect co-ordination for the follow through. I think he's a better left-hander than Sobers and as a fielder he's brilliant anywhere.

The final place is for the all-rounder. Wilfred Rhodes? A

very great slow bowler but a self-made, limited batsman and just an adequate fielder. Keith Miller? A fine slip field and fast bowler but he threw his wicket away too often by having a wild slog. Gilbert Jessop? Magnificent fielder, a matchwinner with the bat but not outstanding enough as a bowler. My man must be outstanding in all three departments so I have to plump for Frank Woolley. He was at his best as a bowler before the Great War when he learned much from Colin Blythe. He was an orthodox, left-arm, round-the-wicket spin bowler with a nice loop. He didn't bowl the chinaman but was accurate and, as he proved in the Oval Test against Australia in 1912, could be deadly on a helpful wicket.

As a slip fielder he wasn't quite in Hammond's class but he did take over a thousand catches. Because Wally saw the ball that split-second earlier he could take chances and anticipate, but Frank was longer in the leg and less agile so he'd stand stock still and wait for the snick.

But it's Frank's batting that clinches his place. He was the best left-hander over a period of time that I've seen. He was aggressive and with his long reach he could murder any bowling on his day. Once his eye was in, he'd play all the shots—even in the nineties, Frank would have a dip. He wasn't a slogger. Frank played straight and concentrated on hitting the ball as hard as possible whenever possible.

The crowd loved him and he was a perfect gentleman to play with. Whenever Warwickshire played Kent, we always enjoyed trying to think Frank out early on by tempting him to cut outside the off stump and hope he'd get a little tucked up and edge it. Frank would always have a go at the ball and more often than not he'd chase it successfully and we'd be in for a few hours of leather-hunting. Frank was a really hard hitter and I just wish there were a few more of his type around.

That's my side then and I wonder how many will agree with it. I'm quite happy to have three left-handers in the middle of the order. At least there won't be so many stoppages for changing the field. The tail seems long but with all those great batsmen in the early order, the bowlers probably wouldn't get a bat anyway. And don't forget Harold Larwood once hit 98 against the Aussies in a Test! I think it'll be a good side in the field—there's Hammond and Woolley in the slips with Sobers on hand if necessary and on the offside there's Bradman, Hobbs, and Lloyd. I'd have to hide Grimmett (possibly mid-on) and Barney (mid-off) but Sutcliffe and Larwood were good, safe fielders anywhere.

My skipper would be Bradman; I admired his self-discipline and standards of behaviour. Mind you, I don't attach much significance to the art of captaincy. I think it's a bit of a mystique. You're a great skipper if the side's doing well and a b.f. if it's struggling—yet cricket's not as simple as that. My two umpires would be Frank Chester and Joe Hardstaff senior—both former players, both extremely honest and fair.

So here's the batting order of Tiger Smith's all-time eleven . . .

> HOBBS
> SUTCLIFFE
> BRADMAN (Capt)
> HAMMOND
> WOOLLEY
> LLOYD
> SOBERS
> OLDFIELD (Wk)
> LARWOOD
> BARNES
> GRIMMETT

I wouldn't mind seeing that side in action. It would bring back many happy memories. Just for fun, I've picked a reserve eleven . . .

> HUTTON (Capt)
> WOODFULL
> HEADLEY

104

COMPTON
TRUMPER
PROCTER
RHODES
LILLEY (Wk)
HORDERN
TRUEMAN
HALL

As I look at both these sides I'm struck by the players I've left out—W. G. Grace, Monty Noble, Charlie Macartney, Herby Taylor, George Hirst, Bill Ponsford, Clyde Walcott, Frank Worrell, Jim Laker, Dennis Lillee and many more. It's been a difficult job and I've enjoyed setting the various merits of the players on my short list of fifty.

12
CRICKET TODAY

I may not be far off my century but I still watch and love my cricket. On a fine day and if Warwickshire are at home you'll find Tiger in his 'cage' at Edgbaston keeping a fatherly eye on proceedings. I may not like everything I see on the field, but old habits die hard and it's a great thrill to see men playing for their county whom I helped when they were just boys—people like Dennis Amiss, Neal Abberley and David Brown. And when I meet up with a few old-timers the years roll back and the yarns flow . . .

Warwickshire have been marvellous to me since I retired from coaching. There were some bad times when I was a player but the friendship and hospitality I've received from officials like Les Deakins and Alan Smith and all the members and players has been first-rate and more than made up for earlier problems. I can honestly say my life has never been happier or more contented—but I can still growl a bit when I want to . . .

As I look at the lot of today's first-class cricketers, I think how lucky they are, yet then again I'm sure they didn't have the fun we had in my day. Cricket's like a factory now. There's too much talking about money and although it's right and proper that a cricketer should have some security, it's easy to ignore the fact that many of them don't deserve such riches.

Very few batsmen excited me in the 'seventies—there's Clive Lloyd, Viv and Barry Richards, Mike Procter, Rohan Kanhai, but apart from them, the cupboard's bare. These overseas players excite me because they're naturals: their heads aren't cluttered up with theories, they know a half-volley when they see one. As for English batsmen it's a terrible period: most of the Test players are just ordinary county batsmen and apart from Gower of Leicestershire and young Humpage of Warwickshire I can't see any young, natural lads coming through.

I don't envy the England selectors trying to pick a side. They could choose any eleven from about forty and it would be the same mediocre standard whereas in my day as a player and umpire you could choose at least three elevens of high quality—and before the First War you could pick a fine amateur side to represent England without any qualms at all.

The fielding is possibly better today than ever before but not by as much as you'd think. Men like Jessop, Hobbs, Hitch and Gunn were great in the field and there's nobody today as good, but the demands of one-day cricket have helped to sharpen up the overall standard. In my day the average fielder may have looked slow because he didn't have the modern habit of walking in with the bowler: instead they watched the batsman's grip on the bat and his feet when he shaped up for the shot so they could tell where the ball would go. And that remains a good rule: Derek Randall would save himself a lot of energy if he watched the batsman's grip and feet rather than dashing around.

It saddens me to see the decline in wicket-keeping standards. Many of them are just glorified long-stops. They may take more catches in a game than in my day but that's because they stand back so often and pinch first slip's catches. I long for the day when the keeper stands up most of the time—that's why I rate Bob Taylor so highly. He has all the qualities of the great keepers I've known. He's undemonstrative, safe, always in the right position, never needs to dive and shows great skill when standing up to the medium-pacers. I was so glad when he got his chance to play for England and hope he keeps it for years so the youngsters can use him as an ideal model of what the art of keeping's all about. Both Bob and Keith Andrew suffered from one of the curses of modern cricket—the need to have a batsman/wicket-keeper. Alan Knott and Godfrey Evans gave England great service yet neither had the class of Andrew or Taylor behind the stumps. But because the specialist batsmen weren't up to making consistently big scores, England needed a keeper who could bat a bit. That's wrong, in my opinion. A keeper is a specialist and if he can bat, that's a bonus, but shouldn't be essential.

I'm not happy about the standard of bowling either. The fast bowler dominates too much in modern cricket: the tactics are geared around the new ball—the batsmen are kept quiet by the medium-pacer while the opening bowlers get their breath back. And their run-ups are ridiculously long. Now I know I won't be popular with the modern players for saying this because they say they need to build up rhythm on their run but I think that's hogwash. Too many of them run forty yards and deliver the ball at not much more than medium pace. They waste their run-ups, they stop halfway through, go through the motions for a few yards and then they're off balance when they deliver the ball. Not enough of them run straight; this curving-run nonsense only leads to an off-balance delivery. I'd have some fun with them in the nets if I was a little younger!

I can't see why the fast men don't cut down their runs and help every county to bowl twenty overs an hour. The customers—especially in Tests—are cheated out of at least an hour's cricket a day with the slow over rate. I'm often amused to see the pace they muster off a reduced run in the Sunday League and compare it to their three-day run-up. Very often there's not much difference in pace. Men like Harold Larwood, Kenneth Farnes, N. A. Knox and Tom Richardson didn't need long runs to get pace—they bowled from a side-on position and had natural body actions. And I'm telling you they were much quicker than any of today's lot, and that's not an old man's memory playing tricks either.

The pace bowler is responsible for a lot of slow play. This interminable polishing of the ball amuses me. They say it increases the swing so they rub away on their shirts and flannels all day and hold the game up by dawdling back to their mark while polishing the ball. Yet nobody ever did that when I was a player—Johnny Douglas would sometimes rub it on his arm but nobody ever rubbed it on their flannels. Oh, the fast man would want the ball kept clean and he'd play merry hell when it was rubbed in the ground for the spinner but all the fast bowler would do with the ball was rub it in his hands as he walked back. The first player I saw rub it on his shirt and flannels was Brian Sellers in the 'thirties when I was an umpire—yet the old 'uns could make the ball swerve and seam off the pitch. It would never occur to S. F. Barnes or Maurice Tate to polish the ball, they didn't need to. A natural body action helped them get their movement and pace off the pitch. And all this stuff about the right grip for the outswinger was never talked about when I was a player. The fast bowlers like Larwood didn't know how the ball was going to swing, they just concentrated bowling fast and accurately and hoping the speed would be too much for the batsman.

One thing that's not modern is fiddling with the seam. As I watch some players trying to raise the seam and putting cream on the ball while hoping nobody catches them out, I often think back with a smile to the 'twenties and the tricks Nigel Haig used to try. He always took a half sovereign out with him and as he walked back to the mark he'd raise the seam with his coin. He was found out one day and reported to Lord's. After all, it wasn't the thing for an amateur captain with a great reputation to do . . .

I don't particularly like limited-overs cricket, although I realize the game needs sponsorship. I can sympathize with today's players when they tell me they don't like the 'Sunday Slog' of forty overs. I wouldn't have liked that either. It gives you no time to build an innings and gain experience or bowl to attacking fields. I don't like the 100-overs limit in county games either because it takes away the right of the captain to declare when he wishes and it leads the fielding skipper to set defensive fields in the last few overs so that the cross-bat slogging starts. The 100-overs rule was introduced so there might be a few more results but with the slow over rate, too much time's wasted so that there are still too many draws or mad scrambles for runs on the final day.

At times I do get despondent with what I see on the field. The players don't look very happy, there aren't many characters around and many see it as a job of work. If they only knew that in a few years' time when their careers are over, they'll miss the game and perhaps then they'll wish they'd enjoyed it more.

I'm never bored with cricket as long as I can see good fielding. Anyone at first-class level should be a good fielder and there's nothing that pleases me more than to see a fine shot brilliantly fielded. It's skilful and athletic, and being a poor fielder myself when a player, I find such incidents very exciting.

Is there too much cricket? Is that why many players seem burned out at an early age? Probably, but the cricketers won't seriously say so, because they're getting money from all the matches. They won't bite the hand that feeds because the game would die without all these companies pumping cash into it. One of the best things about modern cricket is that the financial footing is sounder. Several counties in my time nearly went to the wall but things today seem so much better organized and the committees seem more respectful to the player than in my time when I was at loggerheads with many stuffed shirts.

I'm pleased that today's players are given more respect than in the days when the average pro was treated badly by some autocrats who always thought they knew better. The abolition of the amateur status helped: the real amateur had disappeared between the Wars and towards the end they were just 'shamateurs' who worked part-time for the county rather than for themselves. It's right that they should just be known simply as cricketers and that the old class divisions should be a distant memory. Looking back now, it must seem odd to the modern player to think of changing in a different dressing-room from a team-mate, or approaching the field of play from a different gate and getting far less time in the nets because he wasn't an amateur.

I think the Cricketers Association, the players' union, has helped improve the status of cricketers. With two of my old pupils—Jack Bannister and David Brown—heavily involved in the Association, there was never a danger that it would become too extremist and unrealistic and the organization's helped push players wages up, given the average pro someone to turn to when things aren't good at his club and also played an important part in the Packer Affair. The Cricketers Association has helped players to be more responsible, in my view, although it wouldn't have survived in my day because with so many amateurs about there'd be ructions from the pros wanting the same expenses as them.

I suppose the Packer Affair sums up the difference between my time and today. He capitalized on some players' greed for money, a greed that was more important than representing one's country. That's something I can't forgive—I'll be the happiest man in England if the English Packer players are never picked again for their country because loyalty in my book is vital. They and most of the other Packer men were happy to turn their backs on the established cricket that had made their names. I suppose many will think mine is a typical old cricketer's view and I make no apology for that. I can't see what Packer cricket will do for the younger generation of players because the top men won't be around much longer to pass their example and tips on to the youngsters. Cricket's like that, it's a game of continuity and although many young Australians will be coached by the Packer stars, that won't do the English lads any good.

It's all very well to say that Packer's influence has helped increase the fees for playing Test cricket—but in England

111

that only benefits about eighteen who are good enough that summer to play for their country. What about the other two hundred-odd who haven't yet made the international grade, or those who never will? Kerry Packer's not doing much for them.

I'm not jealous at all of today's cricketers, even though some of them are overpaid for the amount of talent they possess. In many ways I feel sorry for them—the endless competitions and the seven-day-a-week grind means they don't often have the chance for a pint and a relaxing chat with the rest of the team after the game. They spend so much time on motorways in separate cars that it must be difficult for a captain to develop a closely-knit team spirit.

I don't think the Press help the players either. They're not very constructive with their comments so that many players think the reporters haven't a clue about the game because they're too busy looking for angles. But if more journalists analyzed the game or a particular performance in their columns instead of bothering with trivia then I'm sure the players would benefit from the advice of the Press-box. But constructive criticism in the Press is difficult because of the demands of space. When I was a player the press reports were huge and much more informative. The writer could develop a theme and create an atmosphere and his reports would go on for column after column. If a fielder or the keeper dropped a catch it would be in the press and he'd try even harder after that because the committee would drop a pro for the next game if he spilled a few catches. How I remember one of my first games at Leyton when Jack Devey dropped Percy Perrin of Essex. Our skipper J. F. Byrne told Jack, 'If you miss another one, Devey, you won't play in the next game.' With £6 at stake for a match, that kind of threat would always concentrate the mind. Today's press reports often don't name the fielder who's put one down.

The newspaper headlines boosting a player's ego don't help youngsters either. There's too much talk about so and so being 'a future England player' before he's proved himself and too many think they've arrived once the Press start praising them. If I were still a coach I'd be booting a few backsides because I honestly don't think young lads work hard enough at their game today. I can tell that by the way they talk to me—not enough of them ask the right questions, they're too happy just to sit and chat about general things rather than specific aspects of the game. Perhaps they think I'm too cantankerous or that it's all a bit too serious but I don't think there's enough dedication. Many of them forget that you can bowl badly, take five wickets and get all the Press praise, yet bowl really well for nothing.

And I don't like the untidiness that's crept into the game. This is the scruffiest era I've known in cricket, I couldn't believe it when Greg Chappell walked out at Lord's in 1977 wearing those dirty brown pads. The players who don't have a crease in their flannels or have red ball marks down their shirts discredit the game. It may sound odd today but we old players used to be very conscious we were representing our counties and dressed accordingly even if we didn't get much of a wage. I used to keep a spare pair of flannels to wear off the field during a game because I thought it was right to look my best. If you don't have high standards in your cricket dress, there's a good chance your playing standard won't be all that high either.

But cricket's still the greatest of all games for me even if I do growl a bit when I see things I know are wrong. When you're my age you can express your opinions strongly if asked and as I've never been shy of speaking my mind, I'll happily pass on any knowledge to anyone who asks me. I've still got hope for the future of the game but I want to see the ball attacked more and the bowlers aim for the stumps regularly.

The amount of deliveries that don't need to be played today is staggering—last season at Edgbaston in a county match I counted the number of wasted balls in a thirteen-over spell. Out of 78 deliveries, 42 weren't played!

One of the main reasons why the bouncer's so popular today is because the batsman won't play the ball outside the off stump so the bowler can afford to attack him. And to someone who played against the Jessops and the Constantines and was captained by attacking leaders like Frank Foster and Freddie Calthorpe, it grieves me to see so much defensive cricket.

I'd like to see the leg-spinner return, to see him bowl to his field intelligently and watch him use his brain. The game needs more variety and although cricket will never return to the old days I honestly believe this mediocre era is just a passing phase. Perhaps I'm being too optimistic, but when the game's done so much for me I can't help wishing it well.

No-one will ever master cricket; at my age I'm still learning, still writing in my notebook about certain players' qualities as I sit in my cage at Edgbaston. It'll always fascinate me and as I look back on all the great friendships, and the memorable moments, I'm happy that the small amount of common sense I ever had was used to play the wonderful game of cricket.

EPILOGUE

We completed this manuscript just before Tiger died in August, 1979. At his death he was the oldest surviving Test cricketer, an achievement he remained proud of. I talked to him the day before he died; although desperately weak, he was still in robust spirits—'I've told 'em, I want hops on my coffin, not lilies,' he said. The last piece of cricket news I brought cheered him. I'd just seen his beloved county beat Worcestershire in an exciting last-day run chase and he listened intently as I related the details of Warwickshire's performance—a rare moment of happiness in a depressing season at Edgbaston. Indeed, the previous few months had been saddening for Tiger; too many contemporary cricketers were dying, for his peace of mind. There seemed to have been a spate of them—Frank Woolley, Eddie Dawson, Eddie Paynter, Norman Kilner and Fred Gardner. He was particularly upset by the death of Gardner; he was just 56 and Tiger was very fond of the man he had coached to become one of Warwickshire's finest opening batsmen.

Behind the gruff exterior, Tiger was a warm-hearted emotional man and each death of a cricketing friend hit him hard.

During his last illness, Tiger would lie there, shaking his head about Warwickshire's results and wondering where things were going wrong. The body may have been that of a 93-year-old, but the mind and the attitudes were still keen and aware. And the fact that in the last week of his life both Dennis Amiss and the Edgbaston groundsman Bernard Flack took time out to pass on their best wishes for a speedy recovery was something that greatly gratified Tiger and his family. It was always a heart-warming experience to see the respect and affection shown him when he sat watching the play at Edgbaston; he was last seen there at the Indian Test in June and one of my abiding memories remains the sight of Geoff Boycott and Mike Brearley listening attentively to the opinions of a man steeped in cricket, a man with an opinionated view of the game but nevertheless with the knack of diluting the effect with brusque humour. His trusty stick would tap the ground for extra emphasis as he punched out his views on cricket, while at the same time managing a cheery wave to any friends who passed by.

His memory was phenomenal; he could recite the entire South African side against whom he made his Warwickshire debut in 1904—'I was the strongest batsman on our side, holding the others up at number eleven!' The kind old eyes would twinkle whenever he knew I'd checked out the facts of a game belonging to a bygone age and discovered his grasp of detail was still enviably sound. 'You see,' he'd chuckle, 'I'm not so bad for an old 'un . . .'

He certainly wasn't and at his cremation, the past and present Warwickshire players he was so proud of all had their own particular story to tell about Tiger. Indeed, it was appropriate that his ashes should be scattered over the turf at Edgbaston, the ground where he was quite simply an institution.

He may have been irascible to those he didn't like, dogmatic on certain issues—but anyone who bothered to get to know him soon realised his bark was emphatically worse than his bite. He died a well-loved man and his family took justified pride in the countless tributes paid to an authentic cricketing legend.

PATRICK MURPHY

APPENDIX

Compiled by Robert Brooke of the Association of Cricket Statisticians

E. J. SMITH IN FIRST-CLASS CRICKET

SEASON BY SEASON RECORD FOR WARWICKSHIRE

Year	Ms	Inn	No	Runs	Avge	H.S.	100s	50s	0s	Ct/St	Overs	Ms	Runs	Wts
1904	3	4	3	19	—	11*	–	–	–	4/1				
1905	6	6	1	60	12·00	24	–	–	1	13/1				
1906	2	2	2	10	–	7*	–	–	–	3				
1907	1	1	0	0	–	0	–	–	1	1/1				
1908	6	9	2	64	9·14	16*	–	–	1	13/3				
1909	10	15	0	167	11·13	35	–	–	3	21/4				
1910	19	31	6	306	12·24	39*	–	–	2	42/10				
1911	21	36	5	810	26·13	113	1	3	4	41/5				
1912	21	38	0	867	22·82	134	1	6	8	33/4	1	0	5	0
1913	22	42	0	965	22·98	89	–	5	3	57/9				
1914	24	40	5	767	21·91	89	–	6	3	44/3				
1919	15	27	2	529	21·16	72	–	2	3	27/7				
1920	28	49	6	769	17·88	80	–	3	5	39/13	4·5	0	26	1
1921	24	46	0	733	15·93	100	1	1	4	35/14	3	1	3	0
1922	29	51	2	1303	26·59	115	2	4	4	29/9	5	0	15	0
1923	26	46	2	917	20·84	65	–	6	4	32/12				
1924	26	44	2	913	21·74	104	1	3	1	34/5				
1925	26	49	4	1461	32·47	149	3	8	2	45/8				
1926	27	36	3	459	13·91	48	–	–	5	36/9				
1927	28	43	2	1256	30·63	177	4	2	2	42/7	5	0	20	0
1928	23	37	1	1163	32·31	173	2	4	1	20/7	4	1	12	0
1929	29	49	0	1354	27·63	142	2	6	2	28/2				
1930	28	43	0	1019	23·70	132	3	2	5	27/4				

Studies of the scorebooks and match reports suggest that three of his catches were taken 'in the field'. They were as follows:

1910: v Worcs at Edgbaston: F. Pearson ct by Smith. *Wisden* gives E. W. Bale as stumped Smith but according to the scorebook Bale was stumped by Lilley.

1919: v Surrey at Edgbaston: 2 caught by Smith in the field. W. H. Harris, an amateur from Rugby kept wicket.

1930: v Gloucs at Edgbaston: R. G. Ford ct by Smith. J. A. Smart kept wicket.

Catches Taken while Substitute

E. J. Smith spent much of the match versus Northants at Edgbaston in 1908 fielding as substitute. In the first innings he caught C. J. T. Pool and G. J. Thompson, and in the second innings he caught E. Freeman. *Wisden* suggests that Thompson was stumped but this is certainly an error.

BATTING MISCELLANY:

Hundred before Lunch: Smith scored 121 not out before Lunch on the first day of the match between Warwickshire and Hants at Coventry in 1912. Smith reached his century in 90 minutes (interestingly the scoreboard and spectators had erroneously credited him with three figures one run too soon). The Lunch score was 157–1. He added 134 for the first wicket in 90 minutes with S. Kinneir, who scored 29. He was finally dismissed for 134.

For those who find fascination in arithmetical coincidence the following may be of interest in connection with the above. Smith and Kinneir added 134 for the first wicket. Smith reached his century out of 134. Smith's final score was 134. The other century scorer in the innings was W. Quaife. His score—134.

PARTNERSHIPS:

The following are the best partnerships in which Smith was involved.
294—2nd wicket with L. T. A. Bates v Kent at Coventry 1927.
266—1st wicket with Norman Kilner v Middlesex at Lord's in 1927.
211—1st wicket with A. J. W. Croom v Glamorgan at Swansea in 1930.
196—3rd wicket with W. Quaife v Leicestershire at Coventry in 1925.
181—2nd wicket with F. S. Gough-Calthorpe v Worcestershire at Stourbridge in 1922.
176—1st wicket with S. Kinneir v Surrey at Edgbaston in 1911.
176—1st wicket with J. H. Parsons v Sussex at Edgbaston in 1925.
176—1st wicket with A. J. W. Croom v Essex at Edgbaston in 1930.
It is interesting that 176 is the highest partnership with which Smith was involved at Edgbaston—and that there were three of them.

WICKET-KEEPING FIGURES:

7 Dismissals in an innings for Warwickshire.
4 ct 3 st v Derbyshire, Edgbaston 1926.
5 Dismissals in an innings for Warwickshire.

4 ct 1 st v Gloucestershire, Edgbaston 1909; 3 ct 2 st v Worcestershire, Worcester 1910.

5 ct v Australians, Edgbaston 1912: 3 ct 2 st v Lancashire, Old Trafford 1920.

5 ct v Somerset, Edgbaston 1926: 3 ct 2 st v Somerset, Taunton 1927.

4 ct 1st v Worcestershire, Edgbaston 1930.

8 Dismissals in a match for Warwickshire.

5 ct 3 st v Derbyshire, Edgbaston 1926: 7 ct 1 st v Worcestershire, Edgbaston 1930.

7 Dismissals in a match for Warwickshire.

6 ct 1 st v Northamptonshire, Edgbaston 1912: 5 ct 2 st v Lancashire, Old Trafford 1920.

0 Byes conceded in large innings:

0–377/7 dec v Leicestershire, Leicester 1928 (0 byes in innings of 63–0, 2nd innings).

0–334 v Somerset, Taunton 1929.

Few byes in large innings:

1–417/9 dec v Middlesex, Edgbaston 1928.

2–543/7 dec v Middlesex, Lord's 1920.

2–433 v Nottinghamshire, Trent Bridge 1928.

Good match:

1–335: 1–216/6 dec match v Derbyshire, Edgbaston 1926.

SERIES BY SERIES RECORD IN TEST CRICKET

	Ms	Inn	no	Runs	Avge	H.S.	100s	50s	0s	Ct/St	Overs	ms	Runs	wts
1911/12 v Australia:	4	5	0	47	9.40	22	–	–	1	9/1				
1912 v S. Africa:	3	4	0	35	8.75	13	–	–	–	4/2				
1912 v Australia:	3	4	1	22	7.33	14*	–	–	1	3				
1913/14 v S. Africa:	1	1	0	9	—	9	–	–	–	1 (not w/k)				

PERFORMANCES IN OTHER FIRST-CLASS MATCHES:

In England

	Ms	Inn	no	Runs	Avge	H.S.	100s	50s	0s	Ct/St	Overs	ms	Runs	wts
1909 MCC v Notts	1	2	0	14	7.00	8	–	–	–	1				
11 Players v Gts (L)														
Eng XI v Londesbro	2	4	1	17	5.67	10	–	–	–	2				
12 MCC v Kent:														
Players v Gts (L, O)														
Rest v Yorks														
2 Test Trials	6	8	1	67	9.57	38	–	–	1	8/4				
13 Players v Gts (L)	1	2	0	6	—	6	–	–	1	1/1				
14 SA Team v Rest	1	2	1	1	—	1*	–	–	1	1				
19 MCC v Oxford U	1	1	0	27	—	27	–	–	–	1				
25 Sth v Nth	1	2	0	16	8.00	9	–	–	–	1/1				
26 Nth v Aust:														
Eng XI v Aust:														
Eng v Rest: Calthorpe														
v Tennyson	4	4	0	55	13.75	23	–	–	–	5				
27 Players v Gts (F)	2	2	1	36	—	22	–	–	–	–/1				
Nth v Sth (F)														
28 Players v Gts (F)	2	2	0	31	15.50	25	–	–	–	–/2				

In Australia

	Ms	Inn	no	Runs	Avge	H.S.	100s	50s	0s	Ct/St	Overs	ms	Runs	wts
1911/12	3	4	0	77	19.25	47	–	–	1	7/1				

	M	I	NO	Runs	Avge	HS	100	50	Ct						
In South Africa 1913/14	7	7	2	137	27·40	36	–	–	1	5/1	3	0	21	0	
In West Indies 1925/26	11	17	0	489	28·76	73	–	–	3	8/4	1	1	0	1	
TOTALS															
In England															
Wks:	444	744	48	15911	22·86	177	20	60	64	665/138	22·5	2	81	1	
Tests:	6	8	1	57	8·14	14*	–	–	1	7/2					
Others:	20	28	4	270	11·25	38	–	–	2	20/9					
Overseas															
Tests:	5	6	0	56	9·33	22	–	–	1	10/1					
Others:	21	28	2	703	27·04	73	–	3	1	20/6	4	1	21	1	
In England	470	780	53	16238	22·34	177	20	60	67	692/149	22·5	2	81	1	
Overseas	26	34	2	759	23·72	73	–	3	2	30/7	4	1	21	1	
TOTAL	496	814	55	16997	22·39	177	20	63	60	722/156	26·5	3	102	2	51·00
RECORD IN TESTS	11	14	1	113	8·69	22	–	–	2	17/3					

ILLUSTRATION ACKNOWLEDGEMENTS

The publishers wish to thank the following for photographs which have been reproduced in this book:

BBC Hulton Picture Library (Plate 8a)

Sport and General (Plate 11a)

Ken Kelly provided all the remaining illustrations.

INDEX

INDEX

Abberley, R. N., 106
Allen, G. O., 24, 67
Altham, H. S., 24
Ames, L. E. G., 100
Amiss, D. L., 89, 92, 94, 106, 115
Andrew, K. V., 108
Armstrong, W. N., 14, 34–5, 39–40
Asche, O., 6
Astill, W. E., 6, 63, 65, 66, 97
Australia, 30–43, 45–8, 83–5

Bainbridge, H. W., 1
Baker, C. S., 22
Balaskas, X., 82
Bale, E., 26
Bannister, J. D., 90, 111
Barber, R. W., 89, 94
Bardsley, W., 32, 34–5, 37, 40, 47
Barnes, S., 12, 15–6, 30, 32–3, 40, 42, 45, 47, 50–2, 85, 98, 100, 104, 109
Barnett, C. J., 89
Barrow, I., 81
Bates, J., 4, 61
Bates, L. T. A., 61, 63, 69
Beet, G., 76
Benaud, R., 101

Bestwick, W., 8, 76
Bird, A., 2
Bird, M. C., 49
Blackham, J. McC., 36
Blanckenberg, J. M., 61
Blythe, C., 55, 103
Boothe, N. W., 55
Bowell, A., 58
Bowes, W. E., 79, 85, 87, 98
Boycott, G., 100, 116
Bradman, D. G., 83–5, 97, 104
Braund, L. C., 12, 18, 76
Brearley, M. J., 116
Brearley, W., 8, 13, 45
Brown, D. J., 89, 93, 94, 106, 111
Brown, G., 58, 67, 87
Brown, W. A., 84–5
Burrows, R. O., 8, 76
Butt, H. R., 6
Byrne, J. F., 3–4, 11, 24, 71, 112

Cadman, S., 6
Calthorpe, F. S. G., 56, 58–9, 61, 63–4, 73, 114
Cameron, H. B., 82
Canning, V. H. D., 94
Carr, A. W., 66–7
Carter, H., 35, 39, 42
Cartwright, T. W., 89–90, 94

Chapman, A. P. F., 66
Chappell, G. S., 113
Charlesworth, C., 23–4, 26–7
Chester, F., 76–9, 85, 87, 104
Cliff, A. T., 21
Coleman, W., 18
Compton, D. C. S., 83, 102, 105
Constantine, L. S., 62–3, 81, 114
Copson, W. H., 79
Cotter, A., 37, 39, 42, 102
Cowie, J., 83
Cranmer, P., 89
Crawford, J. N., 15
Crawley, L. G., 63
Crockett, R., 36
Crump, B. S., 94

Daer, A. G., 86
Dalmeny, (Lord), 12
Davidson, A. K., 20, 100
Davies, D., 62
Dawson, E. W., 80, 115
Deakins, L. T., 89, 92, 106
Dean, H., 46, 47
Denton, D., 19, 27
Devey, J., 112
Difford, I., 50–1
Diver, E. J., 9
D'Oliveira, B. L., 42
Donnelly, M. P., 83
Douglas, J. W. H. T., 31, 33–4, 39, 41–9, 50–3, 77, 94, 109
Drake, A., 20
Duckworth, G., 80

Eastman, L. C., 86
Edrich, W. J., 85
Elder, J., 35

Essex, 9, 72, 85–6
Evans, T. G., 108
Everitt, R., 11

Farnes, K., 72, 84, 108
Fender, P. G. H., 78–9
Field, F. E., 7, 24–6, 86
Fielder, A., 7–8
Findlay, W., 79
Fingleton, J. H., 85
Fishwick, T. S., 18
Flack, B., 115
Flavell, J. A., 94
Foster, F. R., 6–7, 11, 18–21, 26–8, 34–6, 40, 42, 45, 47, 49, 67, 114
Foster, H. K., 20
Fox, J., 58
Fry, C. B., 6, 12, 13, 20, 28, 45–7

Gaines, L., 78
Gardner, F. C., 91, 115
Geary, G., 67, 78, 97
Gibb, P. A., 86
Gibbons, H. H. I., 62
Gill, G. C., 8
Gilligan, A. E. R., 59–61, 67
Gimblett, H., 89
Glamorgan, 62
Goddard, T. W., 83, 99
Gover, A. R., 77
Gower, D. I., 107
Grace, W. G., 12–3, 105
Gray, L. H., 86
Greenwood, F. E., 75
Gregory, R., 78
Gregory, S. E., 40, 45, 50
Griffith, S. C., 81
Grimmett, C. V., 85, 101, 104

Gunn, G., 16–17, 33, 35–6, 102, 107

Haig, N. E., 62, 109
Hall, W. W., 105
Hammond, W. R., 63–5, 79, 84–5, 94, 98–9, 104
Hampshire, 57–9, 74
Hands, W. C., 29
Hardinge, H. T. W., 59
Hardstaff, J., 6, 83, 104
Hargreave, S., 3–5, 23–4, 67
Hartigan, G. P. D., 52
Hawke (Lord), 11
Hayward, T. W., 7, 28
Hazlitt, G. R., 46
Headley, G. E., 81, 104
Heane, G. F. H., 79
Hearne, J. T., 6, 15, 35, 50, 51, 66
Hendren, E., 66
Higgs, K., 94
Higson, T. A., 82
Hill, C., 21, 32–40
Hirst, G. H., 20, 105
Hitch, J. W., 33, 42, 107
Hobbs, J. B., 13, 15, 28, 30, 32–40, 45–7, 50, 60–3, 79, 94, 96–7, 104, 107
Hollies, W. E., 98
Holmes, E. R. T., 82
Holmes, P., 60, 63–4, 85–6
Hordern, H. V., 17, 32–3, 35–9, 105
Horner, N. F., 93
Howell, H., 57–9
Hubble, J. C., 7
Huish, F. E., 7
Humpage, G. W., 107
Hutchings, K. L., 55
Hutton, L., 82, 86, 97, 104

Iremonger, J., 32, 42

Jameson, J. A., 89, 94
Jameson, T. O., (Capt.), 65
Jardine, D. R., 81
Jeeves, P., 54
Jessop, G. L., 7, 13–4, 45, 63, 103, 107, 114
Jones, A. O., 17

Kanhai, R. B., 106
Keeton, W. W., 82
Kelleway, C., 34, 46, 55
Kemp-Welch, G. D., 69
Kennedy, A. S., 6, 58–9, 74, 97
Kent, 9, 59
Kenyon, D., 59
Killick, E. T., 78
Kilner, N., 61, 67, 115
Kilner, R., 63–4
King, J. H., 76
Kinneir, S. P., 25–8, 32
Knott, A. P. E., 108
Knox, N. A., 7–8, 108
Kotze, J. J., 3

Laker, J. C., 105
Lancashire, 59, 80
Larwood, H., 13, 67, 80–1, 97, 101, 104, 108, 109
Laver, F., 14, 38
Lee, J., 74
Leicestershire, 78
Levick (Major), 63
Leyland, M., 82, 86
Lillee, D. K., 95, 105
Lilley, A. A., 4–7, 18–19, 21, 23–4, 27, 100, 105
Livsey, W. H., 58

Index

Llewellyn, C. B., 12
Lloyd, C. H., 102, 104, 106

Macartney, C. G., 39, 45, 47, 105
Macauley, G. G., 25, 60, 67, 74
Maclaren, A. G., 18, 42
Mailey, A. A., 97, 101
Martindale, E. A., 81
Mason, J. R., 1
Matthews, T. J., 39
McAlister, P. A., 38–9
McCormick, E. L., 84
McDonald, E. A., 17, 56, 97, 102
Mead, C. P., 21, 28, 44, 50, 58
Mercer, J., 62
Middlesex, 11, 86–7
Milburn, C., 94
Miller, K. R., 103
Minnett, R. B., 15, 48
Mitchell, F., 45
Mitchell, T. B., 82
Mitchell-Innes, N. S., 82
Murrell, H. R., 26, 44

New Zealand, 82–3
Newman, J., 6, 59, 62, 97
Noble, M. A., 105
Nourse, A. W., 45
Nunes, R. K., 63

Oates, T. W., 76
Old, C. M., 99
Oldfield, W. A., 100–1, 104
O'Reilly, W. J., ('Tiger') 84–5, 99, 101

Packer, K., 40, 111

Paine, G. E., 62
Parker, C. W. L., 99
Parker, G. M., 61
Parker, C. H., 61
Parks, J. H., 80
Parsons, J. H., 24–6, 59–60, 62, 69, 71
Pawley, (Major), 15
Paynter, E., 82, 84–5, 115
Perrin, P. A., 112
Phillips, J., 23
Ponsford, W. H., 105
Procter, M. J., 105, 106

Quaife, W., 3, 9, 22–3, 58, 60, 66, 70, 94

Ramadhin, S., 33
Randall, D. W., 107
Ranjitsinhji, K. S., 6
Ransford, V., 32, 35, 38–9
Reeves, W., 76–7, 82
Relf, A. E., 13, 50, 52
Rhodes, W., 27–8, 36–8, 46, 50–2, 61, 94, 102, 105
Richards, B. A., 95, 106
Richards, I. V. A., 106
Richardson, T., 108
Robertson, J. D., 76
Robey, G., 6
Robins, R. W. V., 24, 75, 77, 86
Robinson, D. C., 49
Robinson, E., 88
Root, C. F., 63
Ryder, R. V., 2, 4–5, 57–8, 69–73

Santall, F. R., 58, 69–70
Santall, S., 22, 25–7, 70

Scott, O. C., 62
Sellers, A. B., 86–7, 109
Sewell, E. H. D., 27, 82
Shaw, A., 10
Sheffield, 72
Sidwell, T. E., 80
Sinclair, J. H., 3
Skelding, A., 8, 76–8
Smart, J., 58, 60, 72
Smith, A. C., 106
Smith, C. I. J., 86
Smith, E. J. ('Tiger')
   Benefit in 1922, 59–60
   Captain of the Players v. the
     Gentlemen, 62
   Career figures, 117–21
   Final game in first-class
     cricket, 72
   First century in first-class
     cricket, 28
   First match for
     Warwickshire, 3
   Joins Lord's ground staff,
     5–6
   1911—a memorable year, 26
   1911/12 tour to Australia,
     30–43
   1913/14 tour to South Africa,
     49–53
   1925/26 tour to West Indies,
     63–6
   Origin of the nickname
     'Tiger', 4
   Playing for England in the
     1912 Triangular
     Tournament, 44–8
   Partnership with Frank
     Foster, 7, 20–1, 32
   Relationship with Dick
     Lilley, 19
   Relationship with R. V.
     Ryder, 69–71, 73

   Selected for England tour to
     Australia, 28
   Smith's first Test, 33
   Smith's last Test, 52
   Umpiring in first-class
     cricket, 74–88
   Warwickshire Coach, 89–95
Smith, ('Razor'), 28
Smith, T. D. B., 90
Snary, H. C., 80
Sobers, G. S., 20, 99–100, 104
Somerset, 74
South Africa, 45, 49–53, 60–1,
   81–2
Spooner, R. H., 6, 28, 45
Spooner, R. T., 94
Stewart, W. J., 89–91
Storer, H., 18
Street, A. E., 71
Strudwick, H., 7, 26, 28, 31,
   49–51, 53, 67
Surrey, 79
Sussex, 9, 59
Sutcliffe, H., 60, 85, 86, 97, 104

Tancred, L. J., 3
Tarrant, F. A., 6
Tate, M. W., 59–60, 67, 97, 109
Taylor, D. D., 89, 91–4
Taylor, H. W., 45–6, 52, 61,
   105
Taylor, R. W., 107
Tennyson, L., 49–50, 52–3,
   58–9, 62–3, 65
Thomson, J. R., 95
Trueman, F. S., 105
Trumper, V. T., 14–5, 30,
   33–4, 38–9, 55, 97, 105
Turnbull, M. J., 79
Tyldesley, J. T., 7

Index

Underwood, D. L., 42

Vaughton, H., 3
Verity, H., 80, 98
Vine, J., 32, 37
Vivian, H. G., 83
Voce, W., 80–1

Waddington, A., 22
Walcott, C., 105
Walden, F., 20, 75
Walters, C., 80
Warner, P., 21, 28–9, 31–3, 38, 40, 44, 67, 75, 85
Warren, A., 8, 47
West Indies, 62–6, 81, 85

White, A., (Sir), 27
White, (Butch), 94
White, J., 3, 98
Willis, R., 56
Wood, G., 60
Woodfull, W. M., 97, 104
Woolley, F., 28, 36, 40, 46, 50, 59, 67, 103–4, 115
Worrell, F., 105
Wright, D., 85, 98, 101
Wright, L. G., 6
Wyatt, R., 56–7, 69, 79, 82

Yorkshire, 20, 57, 60, 85–7

Zulch, W., 52